MAKE YOUR OWN GYM

MAKE YOUR OWN GYM

Indoor-Outdoor Sports Equipment

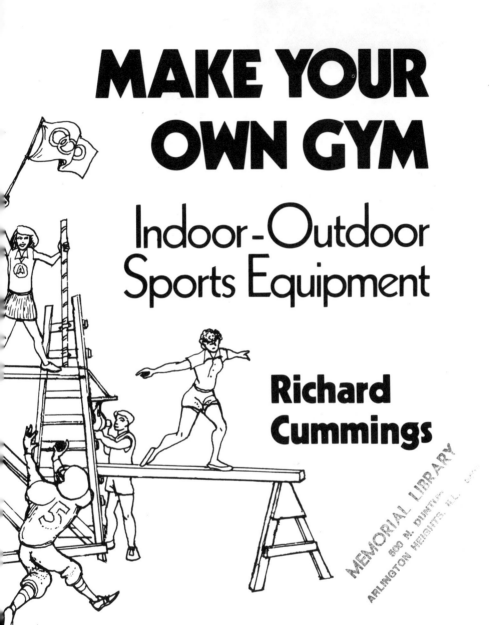

Richard Cummings

David McKay Company, Inc.
New York

Library of Congress Cataloging in Publication Data

Gardner, Richard M.
  Make your own gym.

    Bibliography: p. 109
    Includes index.
    SUMMARY: Diagrams and instructions for building
more than 50 projects, including basketball and
archery targets, bowling greens, tetherballs,
batting and running devices, boxing and tennis
practice gear, gymnastics and balancing equipment,
a sports wall, and a gymnasium unit for small
children.
    1. Athletics—Apparatus and equipment—Design
and construction. 2. Recreation—Apparatus and
equipment—Design and construction. [1. Athletics—
Apparatus and equipment—Design and construction.
2. Recreation—Apparatus and equipment—Design and
construction. 3. Handicraft] I. Title.
GV475.G37   688.7'6   78-5201
ISBN 0-679-20800-3

            10 9 8 7 6 5 4 3 2 1

    Manufactured in the United States of America

CONTENTS

TAKE YOUR PICK

In this book are seventy pieces of gymnasium and sports apparatus you can make at home. Some are suitable for outdoors, some for indoors, and others can be used both indoors and out. We have grouped the projects according to the physical activities with which they are associated. For instance, in the chapter on throwing, you'll find instructions for making a basketball backboard and a horseshoe pitch. The chapter on climbing includes plans for building a cantilevered rope climb and a jungle gym; and the chapter on balancing gives the dimensions for an Olympic-style balance beam.

If you have a particular sport in mind, consult the Index at the back of the book under the name of the sport. Under tennis, you'll find a rebound net (in chapter 1) and a rebound wall (in chapter 2). Listed under baseball, are a pitching target (in chapter 1) and a hitting-practice device (in chapter 2). Tumbling mats (in chapter 2), a vaulting horse (in chapter 5), and a horizontal bar and flying rings (in chapter 8) are included under gymnastics.

The dimensions and other specifications for each piece of equipment have been taken from official sources, whenever available.

You may choose to make only one piece of apparatus or you may wish to make several. The pieces of equipment you choose to make can become a gymnasium exactly suited to your particular needs. Ideas for designing your own gym are included in the final chapter, along with layouts for two all-in-one combination gyms.

Although Olympic and most European athletic apparatus is built to metric specifications, the rulers and other measuring devices of most American home workshops are still marked in feet and inches. For that reason, our illustrations give all dimensions in English measure. However, we have included a Table of Metric Conversion and Equivalents at the back of the book for your convenience.

1.
THROWING

A. Basketball Backboard

A basketball backboard should be mounted so that the hoop will be high enough off the ground to make it a challenge to toss the ball through the basket. The official height, from ground to hoop rim, is ten feet, but the hoop can be lowered for younger or shorter players. The backboard should be rigid and solid, so that the ball will rebound sharply. It should also be large enough to allow the ball to bank off the board and into the basket.

The official dimensions for a basketball backboard are shown in figure 3. Similar backboards are used in women's netball. All Olympic backboards and most collegiate and professional ones are rectangular, as shown. Some neighborhood and high-school basketball courts trim off the upper (and sometimes the lower) corners of the rectangle, according to the dotted lines in the diagram. This makes the backboard lighter and easier to mount, but it is not recommended for the serious player.

Notice that the hoop bracket is mounted six inches above the bottom of the board. The rebound area just above the hoop is marked with painted lines or tape, two inches wide, in the dimensions shown. Similar lines mark the outside edge of the board. The surface of the board can be painted white, off-white, yellow, gray, or medium green; the lines should be of a contrasting color, preferably black or white. The hoop is custom-

1

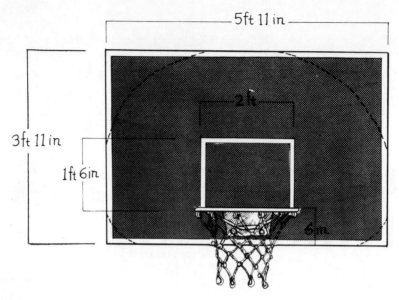

Figure 3

arily orange. The basket consists of a white cord net tight enough to briefly hold the ball before it drops through. The hoop is one foot, six inches in diameter. Netball, which requires a soccer ball rather than a basketball, uses a hoop which is one foot, three inches in diameter.

Because the hoop must be very sturdy, it is nearly impossible to put one together without welding equipment. A net, made of strong fishing cord, can be knotted together. However, most commercial hoops come complete with net. Therefore, we recommend purchasing a hoop and net from a sporting goods store. The rest of the backboard can be made with materials available in most building supply outlets and with tools found around the average home.

GARAGE-MOUNTED

Figure 4 shows a backboard mounted on a garage or other outbuilding. The top of the board is attached to the leading edge of the roof by 4-inch lag bolts (actually large screws with bolt heads) or large spikes. Keep in mind that the continuous impact of the ball against the board requires that the board be attached

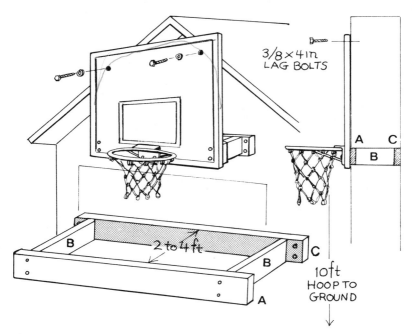

Figure 4

securely. The bottom edge of the board, mounted on a bracket made of pine or spruce two-by-fours, holds the board even with the roof overhang—usually from two to four feet away from the face of the building's wall. Officially, the front edge of the hoop should be three feet, eleven inches out from the upright support, so that a player can come in under the basket for an overhand shot without being hindered by the wall or the uprights. However, a clearance of two or three feet is acceptable for backyard practice.

Use a level or a plumb line to make sure the board is in true vertical to the ground or court, so that bank shots will strike the board reliably from all angles. Otherwise, you'll be practicing in an eccentric situation which will not hold true in other courts.

FREE-STANDING

Figure 5 shows a free-standing support system made of common lumber and hardware. The backboard assembly is adjustable; it can be raised or lowered to suit younger or older,

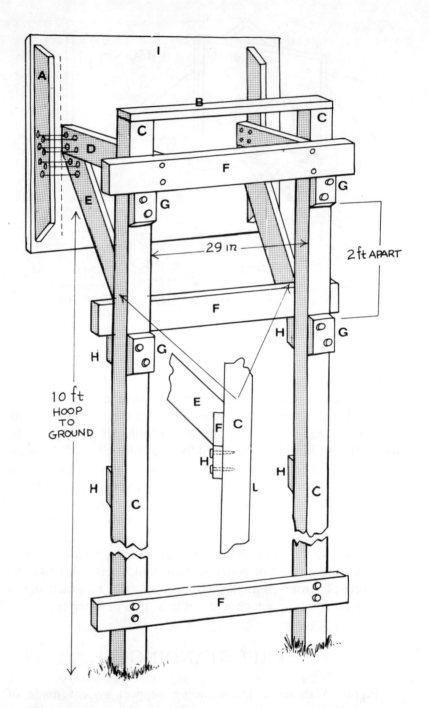

Figure 5

and shorter or taller players. (It is recommended that all players begin, as soon as possible, to aim at the official height of ten feet.)

The backstop assembly is heavy enough to get a clamping action between the cross ties, F, and the 4-×-4-inch upright posts, C. Thus, it can be moved up or down, and will remain in place without special clamping or bolting hardware. If you don't intend to move the backstop up and down, it can be fixed in any one of the positions indicated by the chocks, G and H, and bolted or nailed permanently in place.

The dimensions of the various parts are as follows:

a. Backboard uprights, 2″ × 6″ × 28″ (two required).
b. Top plate, 2″ × 4″ × 36″ (one required).
c. Support posts, 4″ × 4″ × 15′ (two required).
d. Horizontal braces, 2″ × 6″ × 29″ (two required).
e. Angle braces, 2″ × 6″ × 30″ (two required).
f. Cross ties, 2″ × 6″ × 42″ (three required).
g. Back chocks, 2″ × 4″ × 8½″ (two required for each setting).
h. Front chocks, 2″ × 4″ × 8½″ (two required for each setting).
i. Backboard, exterior plywood, 3/4″ × 47″ × 71″ (two required, screwed together for double thickness).

The backboard is made of a double thickness of 3/4-inch plywood for solidity, as well as for the weight that holds the movable assembly in place on the upright posts. But if you decide to permanently fix the backstop assembly in any one position, the backboard can be cut from a single sheet of 1-inch exterior plywood.

To assemble, first attach the backboard uprights, A, to the backboard, using a strong glue and 3/8-×-2½-inch lag bolts, four to each upright.

Next, attach the horizontal and angle braces, D and E, to the two upper cross ties, F, with 3/8-×-2½-inch lag bolts. The inset drawing between the legs of the assembly indicates the manner in which the angle brace, E, is cut to rest on the cross tie, F; the assembly will eventually rest its weight on the inside chock, H. The joint between the horizontal braces, D, and the upper cross tie, F, can be reinforced by the addition of steel T-plates held in place by 1-×-1/4-inch flatheaded screws.

Now, attach the plywood backboard to the backstop assembly at the point where the horizontal and angle braces meet (upper left corner of the drawing). Use seven 3/8-×-4-inch lag bolts on each side, placed in the positions indicated.

Attach the hoop to the front surface of the backboard, then lay the backstop assembly aside until the support assembly is ready.

To put together the support assembly, first attach the front and back chocks, G and H, at the heights desired. Secure them to the 4-×-4-inch uprights with 3/8-×-4-inch lag bolts and washers, two to each chock.

The uprights, C, may now be raised into position for play. They should be sunk three feet below grade, or below the level of the playing surface, and firmly set in concrete or cement blocks (see figure 57). A coating of creosote or other preservative, brushed on the lower three feet of the posts, will help them to last many years. Make sure that the posts are set exactly twenty-nine inches apart, from inside edge to inside edge, and that they are exactly perpendicular to the playing surface. Add the bottom cross

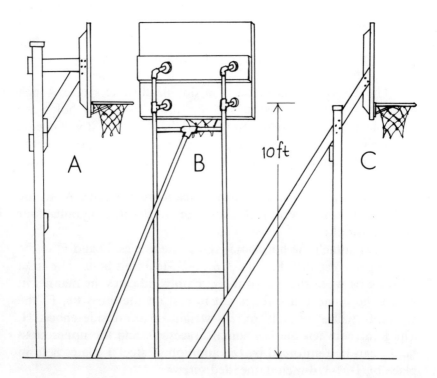

Figure 6

tie, F, and the top plate, B, to make sure that this distance does not vary.

The backstop assembly may now be raised and slipped into position over the posts, with the cross ties, F, resting on the chocks, G. The weight of the assembly will be borne by the chock. Because of the way the assembly fits onto the uprights, that weight will also help to clamp the assembly in place; the backboard will then provide solid resistance to a rebounding basketball. The whole assembly can still be moved up or down.

Other methods of constructing a free-standing backboard are suggested in figure 6. Diagram A is a profile of the assembly just described. Diagram B shows an upright system made of metal pipe. This can be put together with ordinary plumbing pipe and fittings or it can be welded for strength and longer life. The long, rear support slants away from the upright frame at an angle of about 35 degrees. All three supporting posts are firmly seated in concrete, and set at least three feet below grade. Diagram C suggests a similar assembly made of lumber, but with *two* long rear supports made of 2-×-4-inch lumber set at an angle of 45 degrees. These rear support beams are cantilevered to extend beyond the uprights at the top of the assembly, thus holding the backboard away from the upright frame.

B. Target Rings

Sometimes there is nobody around with whom you can play catch. One simple and inexpensive way to perfect your throwing arm is to set up a target ring. Mount it on an upright or hang it from a tree limb or other handy support as shown in figure 7. An instant ring can easily be made by bending a wire clothes hanger into a circle, and hanging it by its hook. Barrel hoops can be used, as well as a plastic hoola hoop, which makes an acceptable baseball pitching target. You can also make a target ring from sheet metal, heavy baling wire, or insulated electric wire (No. 12 or No. 14). Or you can cut one out of plywood with a coping saw, jig saw, or an electric saber saw.

The dimensions of the ring depend upon which sport and which position you are working. A quarterback passing a football hopes to hit an area well within the reach of the receiver—twenty-four inches on the average, thirty-six inches at the most. The dimensions of the baseball batting zone are shown in figure 8. For

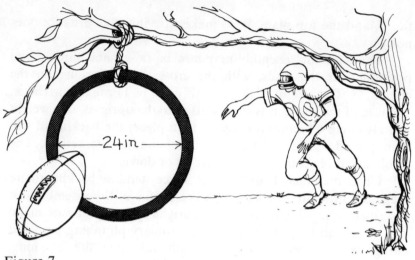

Figure 7

pitching practice, you may want to hang a square hoop representing the exact batting zone. For volleyball throwing and hitting
practice, a thirty-six-inch hoop is approximately the right size. The
same diameter is suitable for a tennis target ring. (A net line,
made of a length of rope stretched between two trees, is also
useful. See chapter 2, section D.)

The throwing distance from the target will vary with the sport
and position you are practicing to perfect. In baseball, the
distance from the pitcher's mound to home plate is sixty feet, six
inches. A football quarterback usually throws the ball a distance
of from three to sixty yards. In tennis, the distance from serving
line to net is thirty-nine feet. this same dimension in badminton is
twenty-two feet; in volleyball, it is thirty-nine feet, six inches.
Archers shoot a distance ranging from thirty-three to ninety-nine
yards.

You may want to go a step further, and incorporate targets
and/or net line into the construction of a target wall.

C. Target Wall

While it requires some extra work and expense, a target wall
has several advantages over target rings. It will stop—and partly
return—a thrown ball that misses the target; and it will trap and
hold a ball that goes through the target.

Construct a wooden frame along the lines suggested at the top of figure 8. Use 2-×-4-inch lumber for the uprights and top and bottom stringers, and 1-×-4-inch lumber for the cross ties and struts. The overall dimensions in the diagram are for a frame which will take three 8-×-4-foot plywood panels. Plywood, 3/8 inch thick, will be sufficient, but 1/2-inch thick plywood is better. Exterior (CDX) plywood is preferred for outdoor use; interior

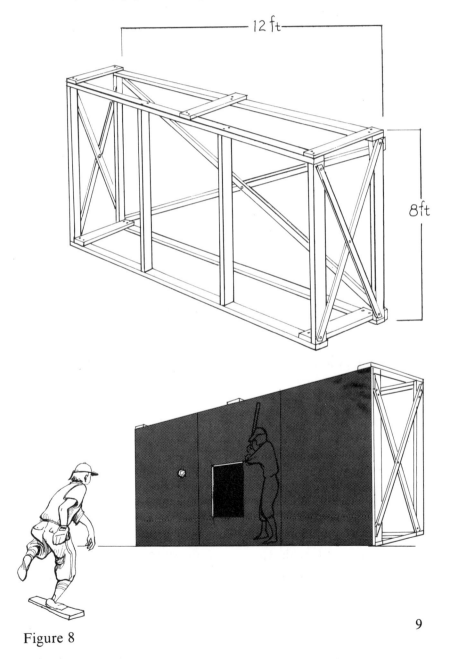

Figure 8

9

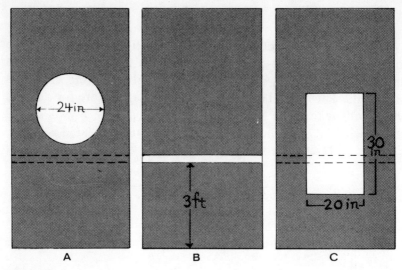

Figure 9

plywood will do for an indoor set-up. Prepare the target panels for those sports in which you are interested, cutting the target holes with a keyhole saw or an electric saber saw. Figure 9 shows target and net dimensions for (A) football, (B) tennis, and (C) baseball. The tennis net line is painted on the panel, not cut into it. The line should extend across all three panels, as indicated by the dotted line.

The figure of a player can be painted in silhouette on the panel, as shown at the bottom of figure 8. This is particularly helpful for baseball, where the knee and elbow positions of the batter mark the limits of the batting zone. For football, you might paint the figure of a receiver reaching for the ball.

Even if you intend to install a single target panel, it should be flanked on both sides with blank panels to stop missed throws. Less expensive chipboard or fiberboard can be used for these side panels.

To trap those throws which go through target holes, enclose the frame in 1/4-inch plywood or less expensive chipboard, leaving one end open so that you can retrieve the ball. Or simply hang a tarpaulin or several blankets over the rear wall opening.

The panels can be attached permanently with nails or screws. Or they can be attached temporarily by tacking them with nails or by installing bolts with wing nuts for easy removal.

The target wall also makes an excellent background for the mounting of an archery target.

10

D. Archery Target

Archery targets are made of straw ropes stitched together, as shown in figure 10. Baled straw can be obtained inexpensively in any rural area. Generally speaking, oat straw has a longer stalk and is more supple than wheat. Other kinds of grasses are supple, but they are usually shorter than oat. Ask for straw that has been recently cut. Pull out a swatch and twist it. The stalks should be green enough to bend; if they're brittle from being dry or old, they will break easily. Try to find a bale that is free of dirt and weeds, with stalks that are more or less uniform in length and thickness. If possible, select a bale with most of the stalks running lengthwise. The longer the stalks are, the better.

Twist the straw into ropes as shown in figure 10, and tie them at regular intervals with short lengths of stout twine, or wrap them in a continuous chain of loops. When you have a straw rope five to six inches in diameter and seven feet in length, coil it into a plump disk thirty-two or forty-eight inches in diameter, depend-

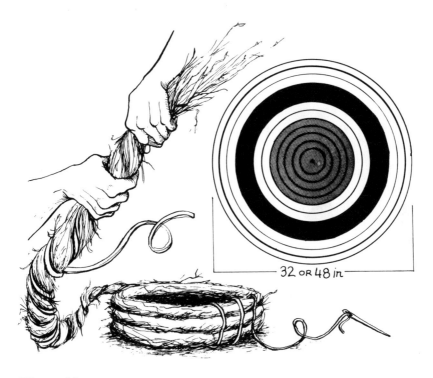

Figure 10

ing on which target size you choose. Lay the straw disk on the ground, and gently but firmly walk on it to flatten it, until it is about three inches thick.

Make three such disks, and then bind them together, face to face, with strong twine, as indicated at the bottom of figure 10. A large sacking needle makes it possible to run binding stitches through the coils and pull the disks tightly together. Loop-stitch the assembled disks around the circumference. You should end up with a tightly packed straw disk about eight inches thick and either forty-two or forty-eight inches in diameter.

Then place a target—a round piece of paper, cloth, or plastic sheeting—on one side of the disk. Mark with ten concentric circle scoring zones of equal width. These ten zones should be divided among five colors: white for the two outside zones, gray for the next two, blue for the next two, red for the next two, and yellow for the central bull's-eye.

Stitch the target face to the front of the straw disk. Mount the target on a wooden tripod at an angle of no more than 15 degrees from perpendicular to the ground. Or secure the target to the face of a target wall (see page 8) with nails and round cardboard washers about four inches in diameter. The center of the target should be four feet, three inches from the ground or shooting surface. Shoot from a distance of between thirty-three and ninety-nine yards.

E. Ball Rebound Net

The purpose of this device is to provide a rebound surface which will not only stop a thrown ball, but will also partially return it to the thrower. Similar nets are for sale commercially, but you can make your own for half the price or less.

As shown in figure 11, the frame is made from 1/2-inch (inside measurement) CPVC plastic plumbing pipe and fittings. You will need three ten-foot lengths of pipe, six elbow joints, and two T-joints. To cement the pipes together, you'll need a twelve-ounce can of solvent cement, made especially for use with CPVC pipe. For the target surface, you'll need a square yard of heavy muslin, light canvas, or elastic fabric. In addition, you'll need forty 1-inch safety pins and forty 2-inch rubber bands.

First, cut the pipe into the lengths indicated in figure 11, then

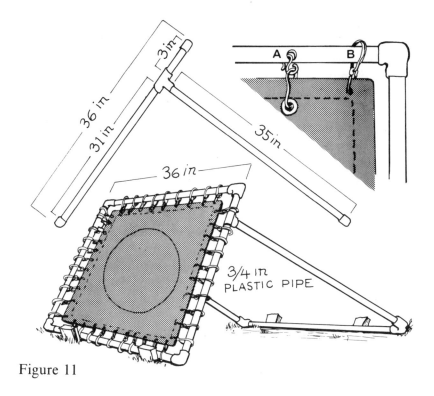

Figure 11

assemble the frame, as shown. Keep in mind that the pipe sinks 1/2 inch deep into the socket of each fitting. Try the parts for fit, but don't glue the frame together at this point.

Next, prepare the rebound surface. Heavy muslin or light canvas provide a resilient surface. For extra rebound power, try to find a fabric such as Spandex, woven with elastic threads. The target in the center of the rebound surface can be a circle painted on for effect, or it can be a circle made of a Spandex-type material sewed to the center of the main panel of canvas. This will give extra rebound to a ball thrown on target. Sew a double-rolled border around all sides of the square of fabric to prevent raveling.

The rebound surface can be hung by one of several methods. The easiest is to thrust the points of the safety pins through the border at regular intervals, ten to a side. Then string ten rubber bands on each of the four front pipe sections. Assemble the frame once again, but don't glue it. Be sure that the required number of rubber bands are on each side of the square.

Next, set the rebound surface within the frame. Attach the surface to the frame by fitting the loop of each rubber band into the loop of each safety pin. Then fasten each pin, as shown in figure 11, B, top right corner.

Alternatively, you can drill small holes at regular intervals along each pipe of the main frame, and secure the rubber bands with S-shaped lengths of wire, as indicated in figure 11, A. This, of course, eliminates the need for safety pins.

Now try throwing a ball at the rebound surface. Since the frame is not yet glued, this will eventually jog one or more fittings loose. But the elasticity of rubber bands varies, and you may find, through trial and error, that you want to change to stronger rubber bands or to add more than ten bands to each side. If the rebound response is weak, you may have to either substitute shorter safety pins or make the rebound surface smaller in order to get a sharper return of the ball. Once you are satisfied that you have the best rebound response possible, glue the pipe and fittings permanently into place with the solvent cement, taking care to follow the directions on the container.

A larger and sturdier version of this rebound device can be constructed of larger plastic pipe. Also, you can replace the safety pin/rubber band suspension system with metal tension springs, available at most hardware stores. However, metal tension springs are expensive. Used springs can sometimes be found at discount stores or in junkyards.

F. Horseshoe Pitch

A good horseshoe pitch or court should be set on level ground. Its target area should consist of soft earth or moist clay to keep the horseshoes from bouncing or rolling. Special pitching horseshoes are made in the dimensions shown in the upper left corner of figure 12. However, common horseshoes are often less expensive.

To set up a court, first prepare the two target stakes. You will need two lengths of iron pipe or solid iron rod, each about one inch thick and at least thirty inches long. Place each of these uprights in a cement or cinder block, as shown. Then pour premixed concrete into the openings in the block to hold the stakes in place.

Next, lay out the court, as shown in figure 11. The square area at each end, called the pitcher's standing area, can be raised an inch or so above the rest of the court. Dig a hole about 3- × -3-

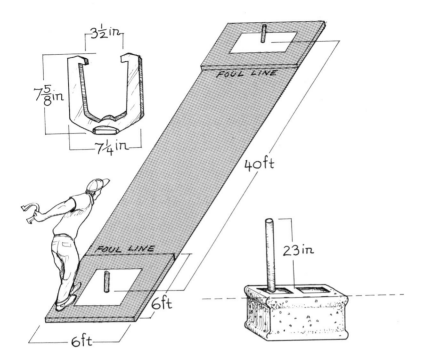

Figure 12

feet square and nine inches deep into the center of each standing area. Set the cement block and stake into the center of the hole so that the block's top surface is about three inches below the level of the standing area. Finally, fill in the space around and over the block with soft earth, wet sand, or clay. Make this surface level with the surface of the court. The stake should measure about 23 inches high. When horseshoes are pitched, they should land without dislodging the stake and without bouncing.

G. Bowling Green

In a number of games, solid and relatively heavy balls are rolled across a stretch of lawn or other smooth surface toward other such balls or upright pins. Ten-pin bowling is the version most familiar to Americans. Canadians play a five-pin bowling game. In flat-green bowls, crown-green bowls, and boules or boccie ball, the balls are rolled toward other balls. A ball, two

15

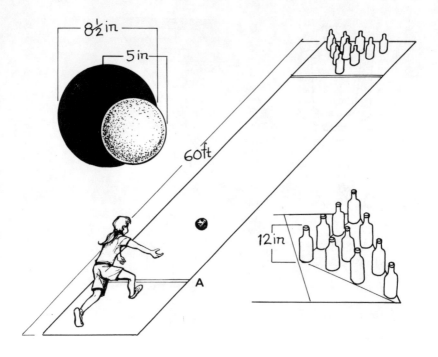

Figure 13

wooden pins of different shapes, and a thick flat disk, called "the cheese," are used in the game of skittles.

Any one of these bowling games can be played (although not necessarily according to official rules) on the bowling green we suggest in figure 13. But it is most suitable for use with American ten-pin equipment. The bowling alley or lane can be set up indoors or out. An outdoor alley should be constructed on a level stretch of close-cut lawn or rolled turf. Perimeters of the alley can be marked with lime, see page 26 or with white cloth tapes pinned to the ground with nails. An indoor alley can be laid out on concrete or on smooth flooring; professional alleys are made of highly polished pine or maple.

If possible, there should be gutters cut on either side of the alley to trap inaccurately thrown balls. For an outdoor alley, gutters may be cut into the turf. You should allow a stretch of ten to fifteen feet before the foul line (A in figure 13) so that the bowlers will have room for an approach stride before letting go of the ball.

16

The official size for a ten-pin ball is 8½ inches in diameter. It usually has thumb and finger holes for gripping. Such balls are made of hard rubber or plastic and weigh up to sixteen pounds. The ball for Canadian five-pin is five inches in diameter, and has no finger holes. Balls for other bowling games are of varying sizes and weights, but all must be smooth-surfaced and have enough weight to roll with momentum. Lead or steel cannon balls were probably the first bowling balls. Wooden croquet balls can also be used, as can the balls which come with various toy bowling sets. A homemade bowling ball can be made quickly and inexpensively from a hollow plastic play ball, about six inches in diameter. Bore a small hole in it, and pour in premixed masonry cement. When the cement has set thoroughly (allow two days), the space left by any shrinkage can be plugged with hard-setting caulking compound, available at building supply outlets. Finally, seal the hole with epoxy glue. The cement-filled, plastic ball will weigh about seven pounds.

Pins are made of maple wood, and are sometimes plastic-coated. If you do not have a set of pins, you can carve your own from maple or a softer wood. The hollow plastic pins that come with most toy bowling sets can be made heavier by filling them with cement in the same way as the plastic ball.

An alternative method of making inexpensive pins, as suggested in figure 13, is to fill ten twelve-inch plastic bottles (the sort in which household bleach is sold) with premixed cement. Allow the cement to dry for two days, then cap the bottles.

For American ten-pin bowling, the pins are set up in a triangular pattern, as shown, and the ball is rolled down a sixty-foot alley toward them. Consult one of the books listed in the bibliography for rules and scoring.

H. Shot Put

Anyone who has been to a farm and helped clear a hay field will have no trouble speculating as to how some of the first throwing games came into being. There are two ways to throw rocks to the edge of a field. Flat ones can be skidded through the air with a side-arm motion (see Discus). Rounder and heavier stones must be thrown with a pushing motion, exactly like that used for the ancient field event known as "putting the shot."

The shot put throwing circle and landing sector are laid out according to figure 14. The thrower must remain within the circle, and the shot must land within the enclosed sector. Official throwing circles are surfaced with concrete, but packed earth will also do. Mark the circle with a two-inch-wide band of lime (see page 27) or with a band of iron or wood. At the front of the circle is a raised stopboard, as indicated, A. This can be fabricated of wood or poured concrete or it can be cut from styrofoam.

The original ball or shot was probably a cannonball. Officially, it is made of solid metal, usually iron. It is smoothsurfaced and a perfect sphere. The shot for men weighs about sixteen pounds; the one for women weighs eight pounds, sixteen ounces. If you don't have an official shot available, you can search in a river or a field for a round, smooth stone of suitable weight.

For directions in laying out the ground markings which outline the landing area, see chapter 2, section E.

Figure 14

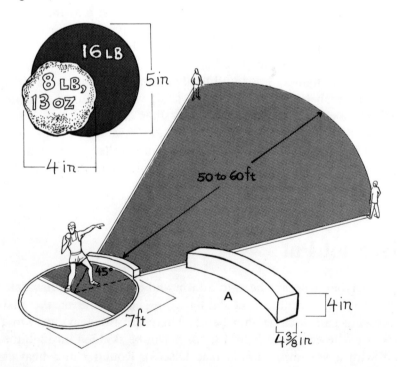

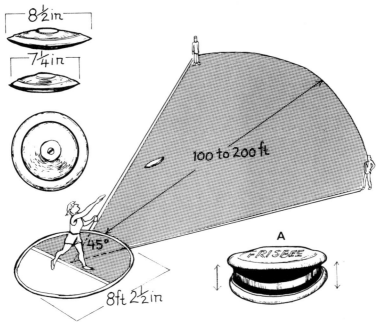

Figure 15

I. Discus

The discus, like the shot, is thrown from a circle, and it must land within the marked landing area, as shown in figure 15. Lay out the discus circle according to the directions for the shot put landing area. No stopboard is necessary for the discus throw.

The discus itself is a smooth metal rim enclosing a disk of wood or plastic composition, with a metal weight at its center. The larger measurement shown in the illustration is for men, the smaller for women. The men's discus weighs four pounds, six ounces; the one for women weighs two pounds, three ounces. If no discus is available, you can make one by cutting a doughnut shape from plywood, beveling the edges to form the discus shape, and inserting a center plug of lead or other metal weighing about four pounds. Alternatively, you can pour premixed cement into a plastic flying saucer or Frisbee. Allow the cement to dry, then use epoxy glue to secure it, sandwich style, to a second Frisbee, as indicated, A, in figure 15. Wrapping this homemade discus with a plastic electrician's tape will make it last longer.

For help in laying out the ground markings, see chapter 2, section E.

19

2.
HITTING

A. Tether ball

Hitting a tether ball is excellent exercise for the reflexes and for practicing all kinds of ball-handling skills. It is particularly helpful to the volleyball player. Tether ball is best played by two people. Each occupies half of an imaginary circle around the center post, and tries to hit the ball past the opponent until the cord is wrapped around the upright. The other player tries to block the ball and send it back in the opposite direction for a possible wrap-around and score.

Figure 17 illustrates the mounting of a tether ball pole, and gives two suggestions for the top hardware upon which the tether line swivels. The pole itself can be made from two-inch (inside measurement) metal pipe and should be eight to twelve feet in length, depending on the height of the players. The pole can be set into a concrete-filled hole, ten inches in diameter, or into a cement-filled cement block, which in turn is set below the playing surface (see figure 57).

For a more secure base, select a pipe sleeve half an inch larger in diameter than the pole pipe and six to ten inches in length. Set it into the concrete base, as suggested, B. The pole can then be inserted into this sleeve for play and it can be removed when not in use.

The tether line should be six to eight feet long, made of stout,

21

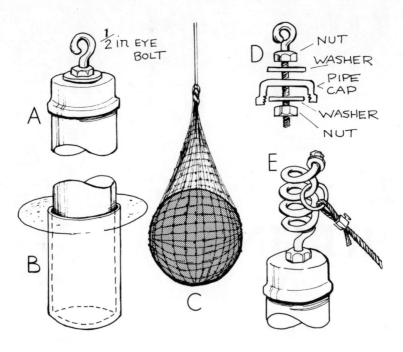

Figure 17

braided cord. Braided nylon clothesline will do. The tether line can be attached to the top of the pole by a 1/2-inch eye bolt, as shown in diagram A. Diagram D shows details of the assembly, which fits into a threaded pipe cap, available at plumbing supply houses and most hardware stores. Diagram E suggests another method of securing the top end of the tether line. The coil spring, which can be found at an auto wrecking yard, is secured to the pipe cap by drilling and bolting or by welding. A metal ring, attached to the tether line, moves freely up and down the coils, but is prevented from slipping off by the nut and washer at the top of the coil. This arrangement allows more revolutions of the tether line before it begins to wrap around the pole, and thus a more exciting game.

It may take some patience to locate a ball with a molded loop for attachment to the tether line. Try one of the larger sporting goods stores, or they are sometimes available in the toy departments of five-and-dime or department stores. Should your search prove fruitless, you can use a common soccer or volleyball and sling it in a fishing net, as suggested, C.

B. Batting Practice Device

There is no substitute for hitting a pitched ball, but the inexpensive device suggested in figure 18 can be a help in perfecting your baseball batting stance and eye. The upright rod is made from flexible 1/2-inch (inside measurement) CPVC plastic pipe, available at large hardware and plumbing supply stores. Cut it into two sections. One section should be long enough to hold the ball at the proper height for the batter (midway between elbows and knees); the other section should be about six inches long. The tension spring, shown in the drawing, A, should have an inside diameter of one inch, and should be about six inches long. The two sections of pipe are fitted tightly into this spring, leaving a two-inch gap at midpoint, as shown in the drawing. This gap allows the flexibility of the spring, combined with the flexibility of the plastic pipe, to cause the ball at the top of the apparatus to give way when hit, and then to spring back into an upright position.

The rod-and-spring assembly is held upright by a base of

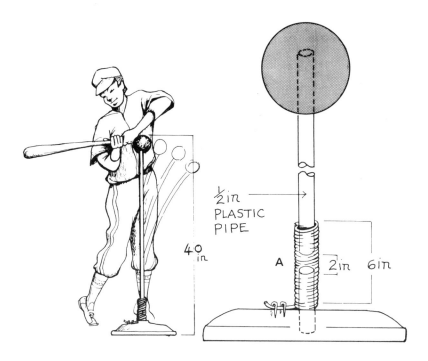

Figure 18

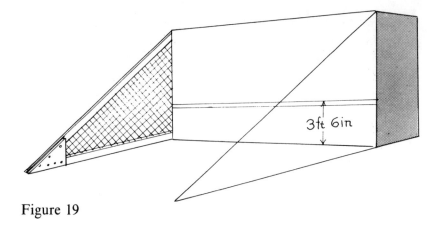

Figure 19

heavy metal, concrete, or weighted wood. Alternatively, the assembly can be set into a cement block (see figure 75) or a block of poured concrete, set into the ground.

A hole is drilled in the plastic or sponge rubber ball, so that the plastic rod can be inserted and glued in place with epoxy glue. Do not attempt to use a real baseball because it will weigh too much. Many dime stores sell sponge balls the exact size of a baseball. Some of them are even molded to simulate a baseball's stitching.

C. Rebound Wall

This rebound wall is helpful for tennis practice, and it serves as a practice court for any game employing a rebounding rubber or composition ball, such as court handball, rugby fives, paddleball, and squash.

The frame is made of common lumber, following the construction plan given for the target wall shown in figure 8. There will be no need to cover or drape the back wall surface, since no balls will be going through open targets. Instead, they will bounce back from the front surface, which consists of three sheets of firmly nailed or screwed exterior plywood. For a firm rebound, 3/4-inch plywood is preferable, but 1-inch plywood can be used, also. Figure 19 shows a white line painted across the surface. This represents the top edge of the tennis net, but the surface can be painted with any appropriate markings, such as a service line for squash, which runs horizontally six feet above the playing surface.

In order to trap balls glancing off the rebound surface, you can extend wings on either side, as shown. These can be made of wood or pipe and covered with wire or cord netting, or with plywood or other solid sheeting.

D. Service Net

Service nets for tennis, badminton, and volleyball are all of similar construction. The objective is to provide side posts, fixed firmly enough to allow the net to be drawn taut between them. Three methods for this are suggested in figure 20. Diagram A presents the official dimensions for badminton. Diagrams B and C show the proper dimensions for a volleyball set-up. But all three methods are suitable for either sport.

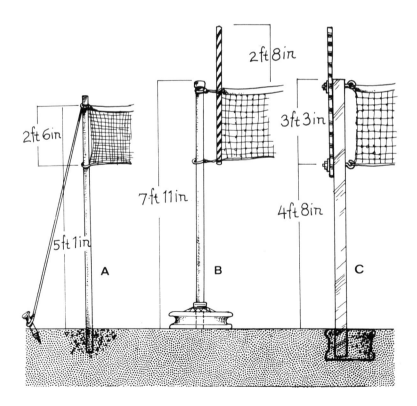

Figure 20

Diagram A represents a simple post-and-guy-line arrangement. For badminton, the post can be made of 2-×-2-inch lumber. For volleyball, a heavier post is required: 2-×-4-inch or 4-×-4-inch. Sink the post into packed gravel or into a base of poured concrete. Or you can sink it into a cement block, see figure 75. The guy line can be made of any stout rope, heavy wire, or 1/4-inch steel cable. If you have room, it can extend from the pole at a wider angle than shown in the illustration. Make the stake from wood, preferably hardwood, or from a twelve-inch piece of pipe or iron rod.

Method B requires posts of 2-inch pipe, with pipe caps at the top to limit rust and to keep the net line from slipping over the top. For the best net attachment, drill holes and insert 2-inch eye bolts to which the net can be tied. The pipe upright is set into a discarded, iron, auto wheel rim. It is then weighted with premixed concrete, poured into its spokes or around its hub. Old rims can be purchased inexpensively at any auto wrecking yard. When the volleyball court is dismantled, the entire pole assembly is lowered and rolled into storage.

Method C requires a 4-×-4-inch wood post, set into a cement block, and secured with poured concrete. The block is buried in the earth, just below ground level. This method is illustrated in figure 75.

Because the attack lines in volleyball extend indefinitely beyond the sidelines, there are striped aerials sticking up from each side post to help officials determine whether a struck ball has crossed within the net boundaries. These aerials can be made of any light lumber or light plastic pipe, wrapped with electrician's tape to give a striped effect.

For aid in laying out the ground markings of the court, see section E.

E. Court Markings

Figure 21 shows the court markings for badminton and volleyball, but the methods are useful for marking out many playing surfaces, including those for field events such as running, hurdling, putting the shot, and throwing the discus.

You will need the following tools and materials:

Tape measure. This should be as long as possible. If you are

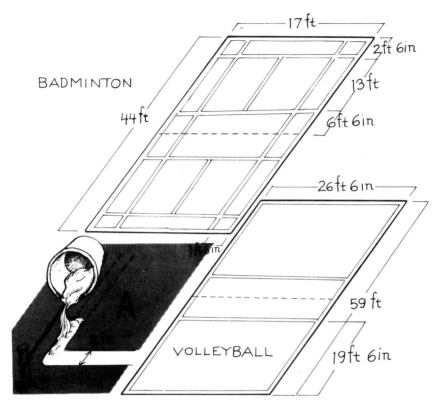

BADMINTON

17 ft

2 ft 6 in

13 ft

44 ft

6 ft 6 in

26 ft 6 in

59 ft

VOLLEYBALL

19 ft 6 in

Figure 21

using Olympic measurements, the tape should have metric markings on one edge.

Stakes. These can be wood or metal and about one foot in length. You can do most jobs with only two, but it is easier if you have a half dozen or more.

Marking line. This can be stout cord or twine. The length depends on the measurements of the court or field, but a hundred feet serves for most purposes. A carpenter's chalk line and reel is helpful, since it not only ties to a straight line, but when it is snapped, it leaves a line of chalk along the measured surface.

A large square. If this is not available for determining 90 degree corners, use the corner of a sheet of plywood.

Marking material. Lime, thinned with water, is the traditional material. However, household paint is usually more readily available. Use a latex or other water-soluble paint so that rain can leach it into the soil when it is no longer needed. Dry, powdered lime or clay can also be used, although they make less durable markings. You may, if you wish, use ribbons of white cloth or paper, instead of paint. The advantage of cloth or paper ribbons is that they can be pulled up whenever you wish. To pin them in place on the ground, however, you will need wooden skewers or nails, which might be dangerous if uprooted or turned sideways by running feet. We don't recommend using them because of the possibility of injury to a fallen player.

To lay out any court or field pattern, start at one corner and drive your first stake. Then, use your square or eye to calculate a 90 degree angle. Measure the length of one side of the playing field using your tape measure, and drive a stake there. Next, tie your marking cord or chalk line to the first stake, tautly stretch it along the line, and secure it to the second stake. If you are using a chalk line, you can snap the line there, and then move on to the next line. Chalk in the entire pattern before you lay down the marking material. If you are not using a chalk line, it is best to do one line at a time, as shown, A. Pour the lime or other material along the ground under the cord. The stripe should be two inches wide. Once the first line is poured, remove the marking cord and move on to the next line, following the same procedure.

It is best to lay out the court or field at least four hours in advance of play, in order to give the marking material time to dry thoroughly.

F. Putting Cup

This simple apparatus can be a great help to the serious golfer who never seems to get enough putting practice. Similar devices are sold commercially, but you can make one at home for a fraction of the cost and in almost no time at all.

The device consists of a tray with a hole in it, a wooden leg to hold the tray in a ramp position, and a cup or canister about three inches deep to catch the golf ball. For the tray, use one of the rubber drain trays made for use under dish-drying racks. Find one with a minimum of ridges on its surface—the smoother the tray, the better. Cut a 4¼-inch diameter hole near the end of the tray that is furthest from the open lip as shown in figure 22. Attach a prop made from a piece of 2-×-3-inch lumber at the rear. Position a tobacco can, a powder box, or a similar receptacle beneath the hole. You are now ready to start putting.

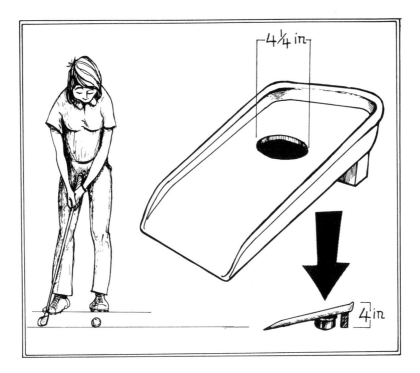

Figure 22

Other materials for the ramp could be a cookie sheet, plywood, or an old tin serving tray. One end of each should be hammered flat.

You can, of course, set up a putting green on your own lawn. In this case, the cup should be at least four inches deep. The cup for the tray-and-ramp putting device must be shallower, so that the ramp will not have too sharp an incline.

G. Table Tennis Table

A Ping-Pong table should have a flat, level top surface, and should stand on steady legs. Make the top from plywood, which is at least 3/8 inch thick, but preferably 1/2 inch thick. MDO exterior plywood is a medium-density, overlaid plywood, faced with a resin-treated fiber surface which has been heat-fused to the

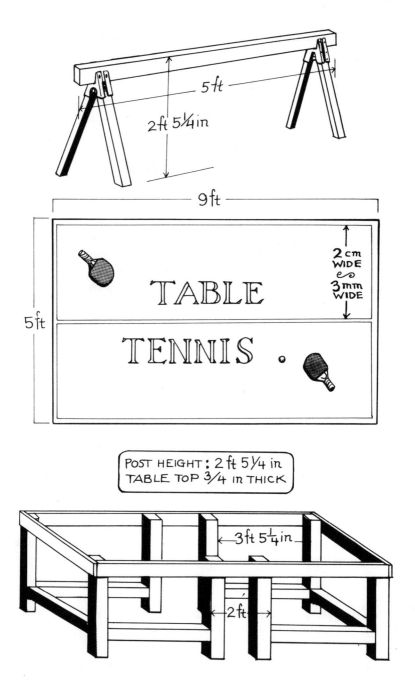

5 ft

2 ft 5¼ in

9 ft

2 cm
WIDE
∾
3 mm
WIDE

TABLE

5 ft

TENNIS

POST HEIGHT: 2 ft 5¼ in
TABLE TOP ¾ in THICK

3 ft 5¼ in

2 ft

Figure 23

panel. This very smooth surface is excellent for table tennis, but it is also expensive. A-D interior plywood will do nearly as well. Sand it as smooth as you can. Then paint the playing surface green and the markings white. As you can see in the center of figure 23, the outside border is two centimeters wide, and the center line is three millimeters wide.

The table top can be mounted on two sturdy sawhorses of the height indicated at the top of figure 23. Metal brackets, such as those illustrated, are inexpensive, and they greatly facilitate the construction of sawhorses. Try to find two pairs of brackets which can accommodate 2-×-4-inch legs, rather than 2-×-2-inch legs.

The table top can be nailed or screwed to the tops of the sawhorses, but if your top panel is level and heavy enough, it can merely be placed on the sawhorses. In this way, the table can be easily dismantled.

An exceptionally sturdy table base—the sort used in official tournaments—is illustrated at the bottom of figure 23. The upright posts and bottom stringers are made from 4-×-4-inch lumber; the top stringers are made from 2-×-4-inch lumber. Members are nailed, glued, or bolted together. This base is not, of course, as easily dismantled as the sawhorse arrangement.

H. Combination Goal

Hitting-and-throwing games, such as football, soccer, speed-ball, and field hockey, use similar goals, situated at opposite ends of a long field. The goals are made of wooden stanchions or metal pipe. The adustable combination goal, shown in figure 24, can be used for all of the above-mentioned sports and others, as shown in figure 25.

Careful study of figure 24 will show that the goal consists of two vertical stanchions, a crossbar, and two vertical rods that hang from the crossbar. Each of the main stanchions actually has three pieces: a top twenty-foot section, a six-foot section of the same pipe, and a six-foot bottom sleeve of slightly larger pipe, imbedded in a large block of poured concrete. The top section is threaded or cemented into a T-joint. The six-foot bottom section is cemented into the same T-joint, and extends below. It is slipped into the larger base pipe or sleeve. Both the bottom section and the base pipe have been drilled with matching holes, as indicated in inset B. Small 1/2-inch metal rods, each six inches long, are

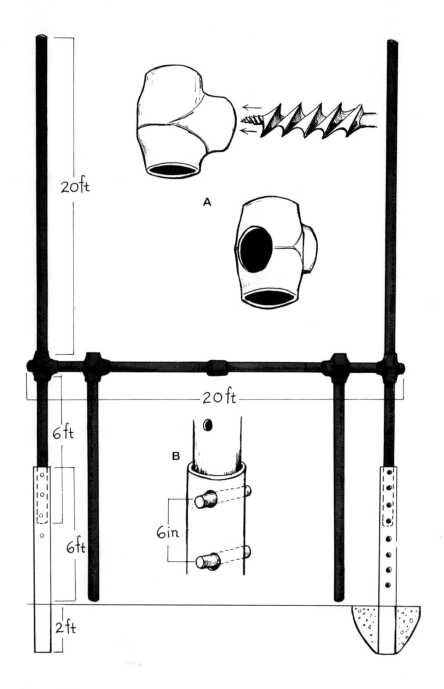

20ft

A

20ft

6ft

B

6ft

6in

2ft

Figure 24

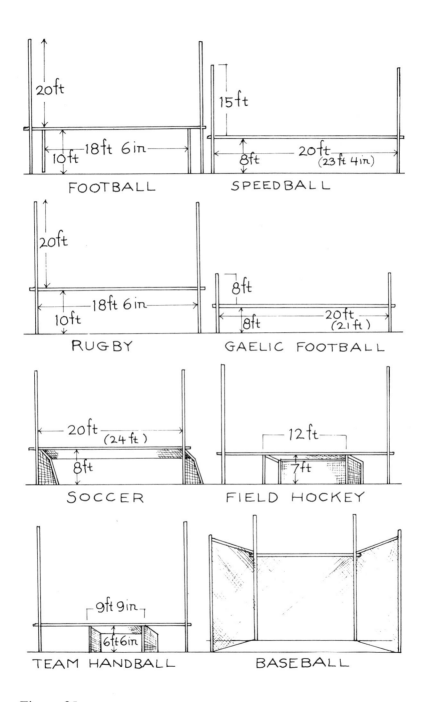

FOOTBALL

SPEEDBALL

RUGBY

GAELIC FOOTBALL

SOCCER

FIELD HOCKEY

TEAM HANDBALL

BASEBALL

Figure 25

33

fitted through these holes to hold the stanchion at whatever height is desired. Each main upright stanchion can be moved up or down to a maximum of four feet, thus raising or lowering the crossbar according to the size of the goal.

The dimensions of the goal can also be adjusted by sliding the two hanging rods toward the center or toward the main stanchions. This is made possible by drilling through the two T-joints so that they will slide on the crossbar, as indicated in inset A.

Stanchions, crossbar, and hanging rods should be made from 2-inch pipe (inside measurement). The two bottom sleeves or base pipes should be made from 2½ inch pipe to allow for insertion of the stanchions. Iron pipe can be used, but it is expensive and heavy. If iron pipe is used, the bottom sleeves should extend a full three feet into the ground, and each concrete base should be proportionately longer. Two-inch CPVC pipe is less costly and lighter, and the opening (shown in inset A) is more easily drilled through the T-joints for the hanging rods. Even if metal pipe is used for most of the assembly, the hanging rods should be made from plastic pipe.

If you're unable to locate full twenty-foot sections of pipe, you may have to join pairs of ten-foot sections with a straight joint, as indicated at the center of the crossbar in the diagram.

This goal adjusts to official dimensions for American football, as shown in the top left drawing of figure 25. With the addition of screens or netting, it can also adjust to the official requirements for rugby, field hockey, and team handball. It adjusts to an approximate width for speedball, gaelic football, and soccer, as indicated by the dimensions in parentheses on the drawings for those sports. The goal can also be made into a serviceable backstop for baseball by adding side wings and screening, as suggested in the bottom right corner of figure 25.

Official goals can be made for individual sports, if the same construction materials and methods are used. The purpose of our design is to provide an all-in-one, adjustable construction which will be suitable for many sports.

3.
CONTENDING

A. Blocking Sled

If there s a single thing the football linesman must get used to, it is contention with other linesmen. A blocking sled offers just the right amount of stubborn resistance. Build the sled out of 2- × -6-inch common lumber, held together by 3/8- × -4-inch lag bolts and stove bolts. Add 2- × -4-inch cross members across the tops of the runners, as indicated by the dotted lines in figure 27. The blocking crossbar, A, should be at the shoulder level of a crouching linesman. It can be padded with foam or similar material and covered with canvas or vinyl.

Sandbags, placed on top of the sled, provide resistance. Their weight depends on the blocker's weight, strength, and determination. You shouldn't be able to move the sled too easily, but once you get your legs pumping you should be able to drive it right across the line of scrimmage and out of play.

B. Tackling Dummy

Here is another piece of equipment for solitary football practice. Make the frame from 2- × -4-inch or 2- × -6-inch lumber, as shown in figure 28. The dummy is made from heavy canvas, cut in the dimensions shown, and double-stitched together with heavy sacking thread.

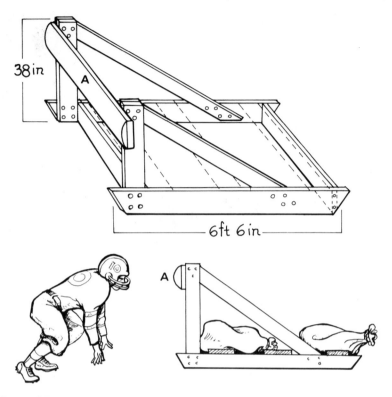

Figure 27

Before stuffing the dummy with cotton batting or rags, run a nine-foot length of 1/2-inch or 1-inch rope through it. Knot the rope at the top, just below a wood or metal collar, as shown, A. The collar, which should be six inches in diameter, can be cut from 3/4-inch or 1-inch plywood.

Now stuff the dummy, packing it as solidly as possible. Then tightly secure the neck of the dummy *over* the disk, so that the weight of the dummy will rest on the disk, which will rest on the knot in the rope. The rope should then be secured to hardware at the top and bottom of the frame, as shown. A good manila rope has enough elasticity to allow the dummy to give way slightly when you tackle it. Braided nylon rope is even more flexible. A tension spring can be added at the bottom of the assembly, as indicated, B. Flexible ropes, although expensive, are available in some rope supply outlets. If you persist in your search, you may come across a length of surplus U.S. Army glider cable, which is ideal for this purpose.

36

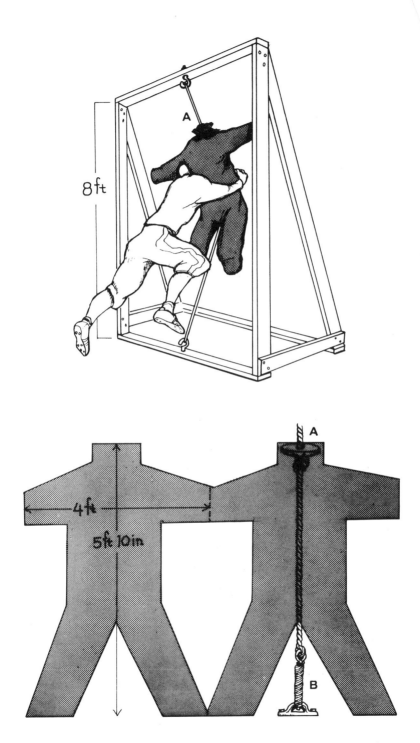

Figure 28

C. Punching Bag

This punching or speed bag is excellent for developing general eye and arm reflexes. The bag, which has an inflatable rubber bladder, is almost impossible to make at home, as is the metal swivel from which it hangs. However, once you have bag and swivel in hand, the hanging and mounting are easy and inexpensive.

Cut the platform from 3/4-inch or 1-inch plywood in the dimensions shown in figure 29. (The thicker the plywood, the faster and more challenging the action.) Using 2-×-4-inch lumber secured with 3/8-×-4-inch lag bolts, brace the platform solidly against the wall, as indicated in figure 29.

The swivel can be attached with wood screws, but bolts with lock washers are better. Take care that the swivel is positioned in the exact center of the plywood, with a full fourteen inches clearance in all directions. It would be best to first tack the swivel in place and hang the bag. Swing the bag in all directions to make sure that it will bounce back. Then screw or bolt the bag in place.

For faster action, lubricate the swivel ball with petroleum jelly or light machine grease.

A heavy bag for body-punching practice can be made from canvas, stuffed with sawdust or sand. Or you can use a strong, cloth laundry bag or a canvas seaman's bag. Ideally, the bag should be tubular, four to five feet long and no more than two feet in diameter when filled. Suspend it from a stout beam or from a strong frame constructed as the one shown for the tackling dummy in figure 28.

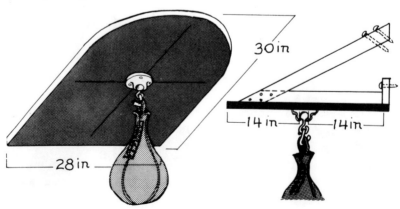

Figure 29

D. Boxing Ring

The construction of a full-sized boxing ring is an unavoidably expensive and time-consuming project. But there is no substitute for the real thing. Since boxers use a ring's ropes, they must be properly padded and firm enough to support and bounce back body weight. You could, of course, mark the dimensions of a ring on the floor or ground. But light ropes and flimsy posts are likely to cause entanglements and accidents.

You can lay out a ring surface in the dimensions shown at the top of figure 30. The ring surface should be somewhat spongy, but also provide firm footing. Closely cut grass or turf are fine for an outdoor ring. One or more old rugs do nicely for an indoor-ring surface, but be sure to tightly stitch together any overlapping edges which might trip the boxers.

An ideal indoor surface consists of a fiber, horse hair, or 1/4-inch sponge-rubber mat, overlaid with a seamless sheet of heavy canvas.

The corner posts are made from 4-×-4-inch lumber. Outdoor posts should extend five feet above the ground and at least two feet below the surface. They can be set into poured cement or into a cement block filled with poured concrete, as indicated, A. Indoor posts should be braced (as shown at the bottom of figure 30) with 2-×-4-inch angle braces atop a 2-×-3-foot base of thick plywood. Sandbags, placed upon the base, should hold the post securely in position. Lead or iron sash weights can be inserted under the angle braces. For additional security, bolt the base to the floor.

The ropes should be 1-inch Manila, knotted at each corner, behind the corner pads. These ropes can be wrapped with surgical tape to prevent abrasion of the boxers' bodies. The ropes are attached to a cantilevered suspension at each corner, as shown, lower left, figure 30. The hardware for each suspension consists of one closed steel ring to secure the rope, one six- or eight-inch steel turnbuckle for tightening the suspension, one 8-inch eye bolt, and two large washers for the hole drilled in the post.

The corner pads can be made of any heavy cloth or canvas, stuffed with cotton batting or rags. They are then fashioned into small pillows, securely sewn, and tied to the corners with strong cord or tape.

The distance between the ropes is as indicated; the top ropes

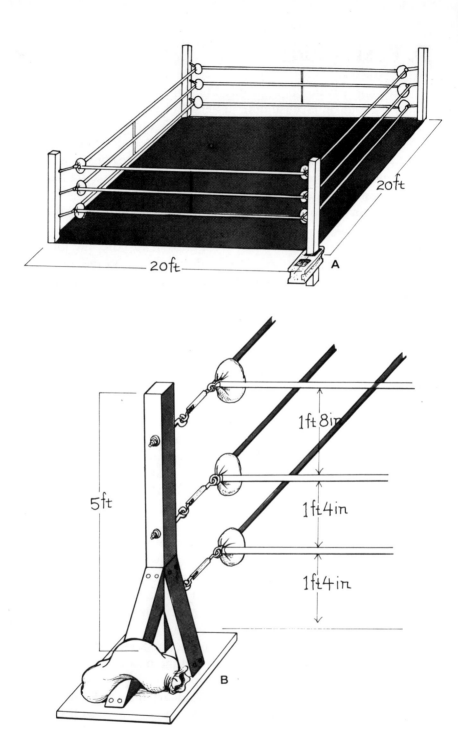

20ft

20ft

A

1ft 8in

1ft 4in

1ft 4in

5ft

B

Figure 30

are four inches higher than the bottom ropes. Each set of side ropes is secured at midpoint with a vertical tie of lighter rope, as shown at the top of the drawing.

If an indoor ring is placed in a corner, only one post will be needed. The three other corner suspensions can be secured to the walls with eye bolts attached to wooden plates, which in turn are secured to the walls with lag bolts.

CAUTION: Under no circumstances should you box without padded gloves and protective body and head gear. Boxing should be done under adult supervision—preferably expert, particularly in the first stages of learning. Boxing is a challenging and honorable sport, but it is also dangerous, as are most of the contention sports for which equipment is suggested on the pages immediately following.

E. Mats

Padded mats are useful for most combat sports and the martial arts, and are indispensable for indoor gymnastics. They are rather difficult to make, however, and require special sewing equipment and skills. Before you attempt to make your own, you should contact your local schools, YMCA, YWCA, or other organizations with gymnasiums to see if they have used mats for sale. Repairing used mats is easier than making your own. Otherwise, seek the help of an experienced sewer with a sewing machine. At best, the mats should be made of heavy canvas, and for this, an industrial sewing machine is needed.

Old mattresses do not make good tumbling or wrestling mats. They are too thick and spongy. In addition, there is always the danger of a metal spring breaking through aged fabric and causing an injury, possibly to an eye. Avoid mats that have any interior metal parts.

A good gymnastic or tumbling mat should be at least thirty-two inches wide and from six to eight feet long. When new, it should be at least four inches thick. With use, a mat's interior material packs down to about three inches. Mats for combat sports can be up to ten square feet. Anything larger is difficult to roll up and heavy to move. If you make a larger mat, be prepared to leave it in place most of the time. Tumbling mats are narrower than those used for combat sports. Narrower mats are best for general use, since they can be placed end to end for acrobatics.

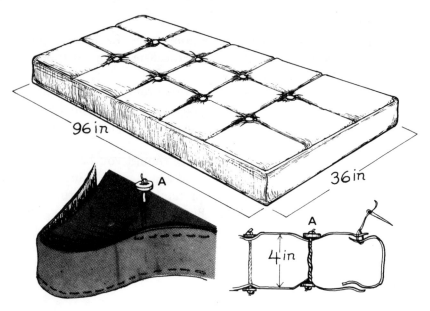

Figure 31

The outer casing should be made from a material that is as heavy as possible. Heavy canvas is best, but heavy muslin or duck will also do. First cut and sew the casing, leaving one or more sides open. Next, insert the packing. This can be made of rags, cotton batting, or other resilient material. Sponge rubber or foam are not really serviceable because they are too "springy," and they do not provide the best balance of resilience and secure footing. Straw is cheap, but will pack to hardness after a short period of use. Horsehair is ideal, but very expensive. Try a local mattress shop for commercial batting, which can sometimes be obtained at a reasonable price. Baled rags can also be purchased cheaply.

Once the casing envelope is packed, sew the open sides, and then tread, or "knead" the mat to make sure that the packing is evenly distributed. Finally, the mat should be tufted at regular intervals, as indicated in figure 31. The tufts help to keep the interior packing from moving about or gathering into lumps. The tufts should be made with strong cord and tied through the thickness of the mat, as indicated, A. At either end of each tuft, secure some kind of washerlike disk to hold the casing surface in place. Padded buttons, made especially for the purpose, are available at many mattress shops and some fabric outlets. Or you might use plastic buttons or large rubber washers. Do not use metal washers, buttons, or any type of hardware with sharp edges.

42

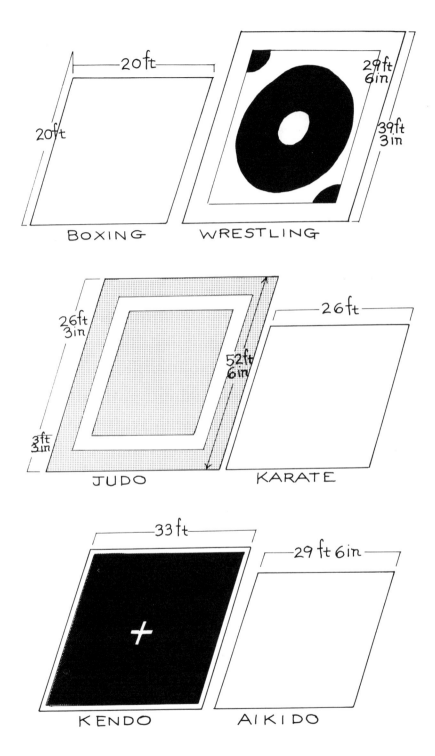

BOXING

WRESTLING

JUDO

KARATE

KENDO

AIKIDO

Figure 32

Remember that you will occasionally be falling face down on the mat.

Figure 32 gives the layout dimensions for various kinds of combat sports and martial arts activities. Some kind of matting is needed for all of them. If there is any question in your mind about how thick the matting should be, visit a gymnasium and find out exactly what kind of floor protection the experts recommend.

F. Fencing Piste

The fencing area, or piste, as shown in figure 33, is suitable for fencing with foil, épée, or saber. The flooring should be flat, and made of wood, linoleum, rubber or plastic matting, or fine steel mesh. Linoleum, laid over a cement or wood floor, is the

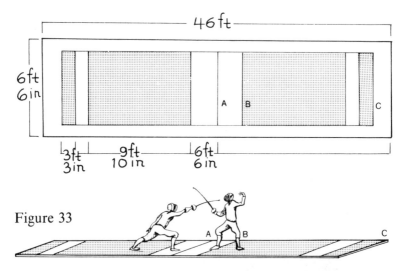

Figure 33

least expensive indoor surface. For an outdoor piste, plywood panels can be laid down according to the dimensions shown in the drawing. They should then be surfaced with a linoleum runner.

Markings can be painted on the runner or they can be indicated with black electrician's tape. A is the center line, and B is the on-guard line. C is the rear limit line, beyond which a fencer may not retreat.

Unfortunately, the construction of adequate fencing foils and sabers is beyond the capacity of the average home workshop. All weapons should, of course, be blunted with rubber tips.

44

4.
RUNNING

A. Starting Blocks

For most track events involving running, the competitor is allowed to propel himself forward to start with adjustable running blocks. Our set of wooden blocks, shown in figure 35, meets official specifications, and is inexpensive and easy to make. The construction of a set of more elaborate metal blocks is suggested in figure 36.

Cut the two blocks, A, from 4-×-4-inch pine, spruce, or hardwood. The body of the device, B, can be cut from 2-×-4-inch softwood or hardwood. The slot in the body measures 3/4 inch high and 36 inches long. To cut it, first drill holes at either end, then complete the cut with a keyhole saw, an electric saber saw, or a scroll saw. Note the 5-inch spikes driven into either end; their purpose is to help the body of the device grip the ground. But they are not always officially sanctioned.

Each of the two hardware assemblies, D, consists of a 12-inch machine bolt with two washers and a wing nut. Loosening the nut allows the blocks to be adjusted to fit the individual runner's starting stance.

The professional set of starting blocks, illustrated in figure 36, is made of steel. It requires metal-working tools for its construction. Notice that the angle of the foot blocks can be adjusted to suit the runner—an additional advantage.

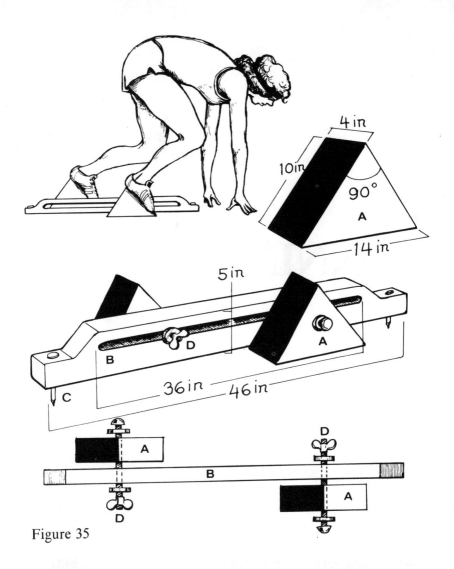

Figure 35

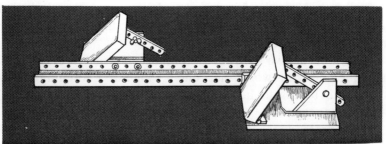

Figure 36

Figure 37

B. Auto Tire High-Step

Here is an old and effective way to get a football linesman to lift the knees high when running. In fact, an auto tire-running course conditions the legs for just about any sport. All you need are eight or more used tires, laid flat on the ground in the pattern shown on the right in figure 37. You can buy used tires inexpensively from gas stations, automotive garages and agencies, and auto wrecking yards. Or you can sometimes get them free with persistent visits to dumps, ditches, and vacant lots.

C. Relay Baton

You can make a relay baton from just about any kind of tubing, as long as it fits the dimensions shown at the top of figure 38. However, the lighter its weight, the easier it is to carry on the run. Official rules require only that it have a minimum weight of 1¾ ounces. You can use light aluminum tubing, with soldered caps at either end. Cardboard mailing tubes are available in all sizes at most large stationery and art supply stores. If you can't find a cardboard tube of the official weight, you can wrap it in plastic electrician's tape until it weighs 1¾ ounces.

D. Running Lanes

Lanes for most running events are laid out as shown at the bottom of figure 38. The starting, finish, and inside lines can be laid down with lime, paint, white sand, or cinders, following the method described on page 26.The outside limits of the track can be the same, but should be marked by curbings, as indicated, A, in the drawing. These can be made of wood or poured concrete. In cases where the track curves, wood curbs are impossible. Instead, an old watering hose, held down with large wire staples every few feet, can be used. But under no condition should you use sheet metal with a sharp edge or any other material which might injure a runner's feet or his body, should he trip and fall.

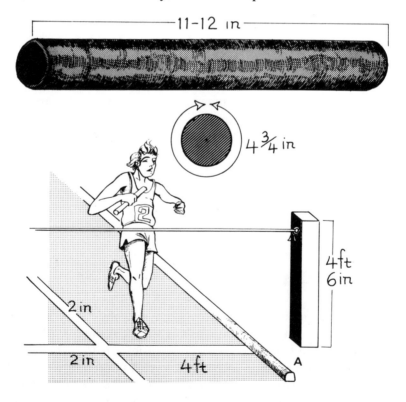

Figure 38

E. Finishing Post

The finish line is marked by two posts, one at each end of the line. They should be set up a foot or more outside each curbing, as shown at the bottom of figure 38. Use 2- × -4-inch lumber, or better yet, 4- × -4-inch lumber in the length indicated, with the addition of at least two feet to be buried in the ground. For a more secure post, pack gravel around the base, and pour concrete on it or use a cement block, as shown in figures 12 and 20. To make the post removable, use a square sleeve, similar to that shown in figure 17. A completely portable finishing post can be constructed in the same way as the boxing ring corner post, shown at the bottom of figure 30, B.

A tape or thread is usually tied between the two posts, to be broken by the first runner across the finish line. This must be fragile enough to be easily broken, yet strong enough so that it won't snap under its own weight or be broken by the wind. Some kinds of paper ribbon are adequate. The least costly and the easiest type of finish line is a half-inch strip of unhemmed cotton, cut from old sheeting. It can be knotted together if the length is not sufficient to stretch across the whole track. Whichever material you choose, try it out before a race to make sure it breaks easily.

5.
JUMPING

A. Hurdles

Olympic hurdles are made of metal with a wooden top bar, as shown in figure 40, A. However, you can make yours entirely of wood, as suggested, B. Dimensions are as shown, with the height, H, varying as follows:

100 meter women's race: 2'9"
110 meter men's race: 3'3"
400 meter men's race: 2'11 ⅝"
decathlon and pentathlon: 3'3"

Strictly speaking, the hurdle should be designed so that a force of approximately eight pounds, applied to the center of the top edge of the crossbar, will topple the hurdle in the running direction (to the right in figure 40).

The metal frame can be made of 3/4-inch or 1-inch (inside measurement) water pipe, either welded together or held together with pipe fittings. The uprights can be made adjustable, with the top portion sliding into the bottom portion. Or you can cut the pipe to a single height. The most frequently used is the men's 110-meter height of three feet, three inches.

The square counterbalance weights at the ends of the legs can be permanently fixed or they can be adjustable. To make such a

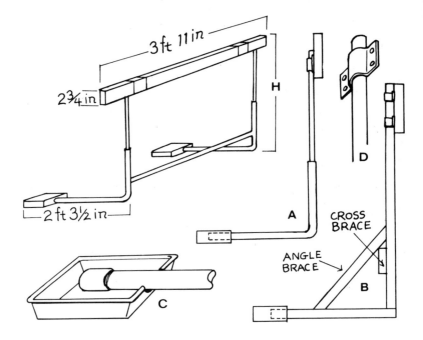

Figure 40

weight, cut a notch in a square cake pan, as shown, C. The pipe should have a threaded or welded plug in one end to prevent it from slipping out after the cement is poured. Lay the pipe in the notch, and pour premixed cement into the pan to cover the pipe.

To make the weight adjustable, leave off the end plug. Prepare a short length of metal sleeve, about one-half inch larger in diameter than the leg pipe. Place it in the pan, and pour the cement over it. The leg pipe can then be slipped into the sleeve, and the weight can be moved forward or back on the leg pipe to vary the counterbalance effect.

Make the crossbar from 2- × -4-inch lumber, attached to the upright pipes with brackets, as shown, D.

The wooden hurdle, B, is constructed like the metal version, but is made from 2- × -2-inch lumber, rather than pipe. It has an angle brace at the bottom and a wooden cross brace, as shown.

B. Long Jump

The purpose of the long jump is to see how far a person can travel in a single jump. The running course, as shown in figure 41, is over 147 feet long and 4 feet wide. The landing area is a pit of sand of the dimensions shown. The jumper launches himself from a take-off board, A in the diagram. B is the take-off line. C is a narrow band of damp clay or plasticine. If the jumper's foot or feet land beyond the take-off line, telltale marks will be left in the soft clay or plastic surface.

Make the take-off board of wood, preferably hardwood, and bury it exactly level with the surface of the running course. The board and the clay band can be framed with strips of 1/2-×-1-inch lumber.

The landing area can be a pit, at least eight inches deep, but preferably one-and-a-half feet deep. Or the sides of the pit can be lined with a wooden frame made of 1-×-6-inch lumber. The pit should be filled with sand up to exactly the level of the take-off board and running course. The sand should be dampened and raked level before a jump takes place.

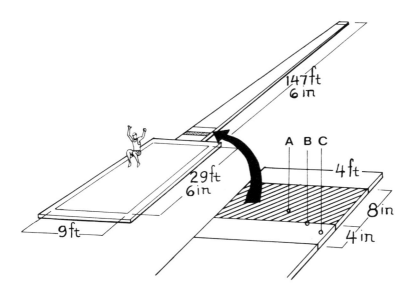

Figure 41

C. High Jump

The high jump is made over a crossbar, set loosely between two rigid uprights, so that it falls away from the jumper when it is struck by the jumper's body. See figure 42.

The crossbar, B, can be a triangular cross-section or it can be round with squared ends. A triangular crossbar can be made from a length of 2-×-2-inch lumber, planed down to a triangular cross-section. The easiest, though not official, crossbar is made from a length of 1-inch quarter round or other light molding.

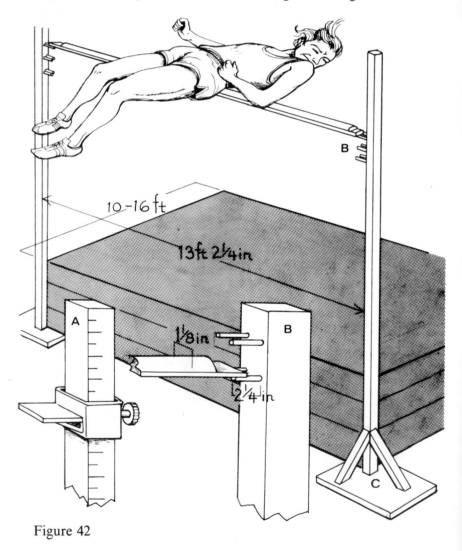

Figure 42

The uprights should be made of 2-×-2-inch lumber, set upright on a plywood base and braced with angle braces of 2-×-2-inch lumber, as shown in the drawing, C. The length of the uprights depends on the heights you will be jumping; seven feet is usually sufficient.

Crossbar supports must face the opposite upright, and be flat and rectangular. The simplest supports are pairs of hardwood pegs, fitted into holes in the uprights, as shown, B. These are not officially acceptable, but they give almost the same effect as the more complicated official supports. As you can see from the inset, B, these pegs extend 2¼ inches from the upright. This gives the crossbar plenty of clearance so that it can fall away if the jumper hits it. If pairs of holes are drilled at regular one- or two-inch intervals, the pegs can be moved upward so that the jumping can proceed to new heights.

A professional crossbar support, made of metal, is shown in diagram A. It can be moved up and down, and it can be tightened at the rear with a pressure screw. Thus, the height can be adjusted to fractions of an inch. You will probably need to use welding equipment to make this support.

D. Landing Pads

A giant landing pillow can be made from an envelope of heavy muslin stuffed with straw, but it should be at least forty inches thick. It will pack down with use, but it should not be used after it has lost its springiness. Use this makeshift landing pad only after it has been examined and approved by a knowledgeable adult gymnast.

6.
VAULTING

A. Pole Vault

While the pole vault is certainly one of the most spectacular of the field events, it is quite dangerous, and it requires equipment not easily made in the average home workshop. It should not be made without supervision. If you make any of the equipment described here, be sure to have an expert examine it before you use it.

The run-up and crossbar set-up are shown in figure 44. At the end of the run-up is a box into which the pole fits. This is made of wood or metal in the dimensions shown, A. The two uprights can be made of wood or pipe, and they are constructed much like the upright for the high jump, figure 42. The crossbar and crossbar supports are also similar to those used for the high jump.

Modern vaulting poles are usually made of aluminum or plastic material. Do not attempt to fabricate such poles because they are made of highly specialized materials.

Pole vaulting was originally done with bamboo poles, and a homemade pole can be made from carefully selected and properly aged bamboo. Its *full length* should be wrapped with two layers of adhesive tape. Improperly aged bamboo can be extremely dangerous if it breaks or splinters. Before using such a pole, consult an informed adult, preferably a high school or track coach.

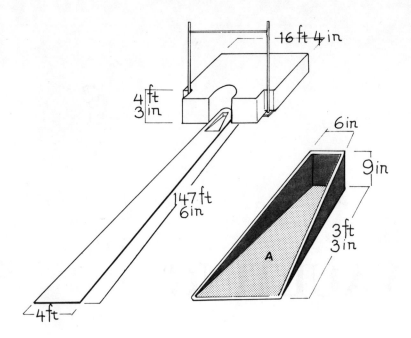

Figure 44

B. Vaulting Horse

Gymnastic exercises, performed on the horse (figure 43), provide excellent overall conditioning and are particularly strengthening to the arms and shoulders. In official competition, there are three kinds of horses: the men's horse, shown (AA) in figure 45; the women's horse, which is somewhat smaller; and the pommel horse, which has two padded brackets at its center, as shown (BB).

An inexpensive and serviceable horse can be made from a length of peeled log, as suggested in diagram CC. Trim the sides of the log, as indicated by the dotted lines. Then drill leg sockets, and insert legs made of peeled log or common lumber. Since a horse must be sturdy and solidly planted on its legs, make each socket a tight fit for the leg. This primitive horse can then be padded with a layer of old blanket or foam and covered with a vinyl sheath. The sheath should be sewn at both ends, and tacked or stapled along the bottom of the horse, where the staples aren't likely to snag the vaulter.

58

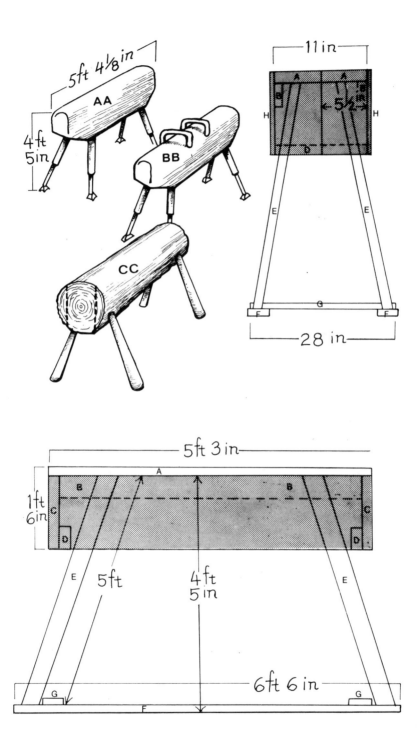

Figure 45

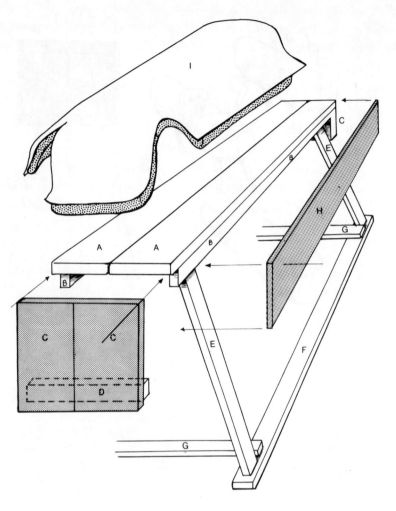

Figure 46

An even better horse, constructed of lumber, can be made by following the suggestions in figures 45 and 46. First build the body, a box made of two lengths of 2-x-6-inch lumber running lengthwise, A, and braced inside with 2-x-4-inch studs and stringers, B, D. The box is covered at the ends and along the sides with 1-x-12-inch shelf lumber, H, C. The box should then be mounted on a base consisting of four legs, E, made from 2-x-4-inch or 4-x-4-inch lumber. The legs are secured at the bottom by stringers and cross ties of 2-x-4-inch lumber, G, F.

The use of machine bolts and lag bolts with washers instead of nails (see figure 5) insures a sturdier and more permanent construction. The box should be padded with a triple layer of blanket or with one-inch foam sheeting, which in turn should be covered with heavy vinyl sheeting, canvas, or leather, as indicated, I. Be sure that the seams of the covering are sewn wherever the vaulter will come into contact with them. Final tacking or stapling of the cover should be done inside the bottom edge of the box.

C. Trampolette

Several gymnastic exercises, including those on the horse, make use of a springing device to give the vaulter a boost into the air. A safe and effective springboard requires expert craftsmanship, expensive hardware, and specially cured wood. But you can make a similar springing device at home—the trampolette, shown in figure 47.

The circular rim should be cut with a saber or scroll saw from good quality A-B exterior plywood, one inch thick. Cut the rim according to the dimensions shown at the bottom of figure 47. Add four legs of 2-x-4-inch lumber, cut as shown, C. Secure with lag bolts, reinforced with small, wedge-shaped chocks glued in place. These legs will raise the rim twelve inches above the floor.

The circular bouncing surface is made from three disks of heavy canvas. Sew them together with concentric circular stitching for strength, and make a double-rolled hem around the outside edge. For extra strength, run a hoop of heavy gauge wire through one hem, B, figure 47. Using a grommet or a riveting tool, punch in 3/4-inch metal grommets at two-inch intervals inside the hem. The springs will be hooked into these reinforced holes.

The bouncing surface will be suspended from sixty 2-inch tension springs, available at most large hardware stores. They vary in strength specifications, so it is best to discuss the project with the salesman before buying. Since they are expensive, try to find used springs in a junk shop or an auto wrecking yard. If all of the springs have closed loops at one end, they should all be strung onto the wire hoop before the hoop is closed. It is best to use a shackle bolt, available at most hardware stores, rather than a mere twist of the wire to close the hoop.

The hoop should then be laid on the upper surface of the

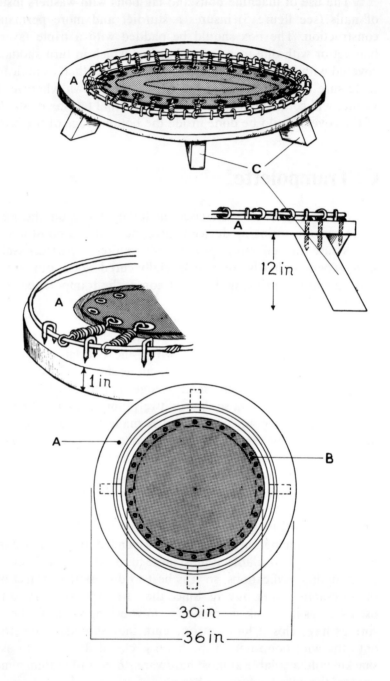

A

C

A

12 in

A

1 in

A

B

30 in

36 in

Figure 47

plywood rim, and secured with wire staples at two-inch intervals. The staples should alternate with the springs, as indicated, A and C.

Finally, hook each spring into its grommet hole and close the spring hook with pliers. Now you're ready to bounce.

7.
CLIMBING

A. Rope Climb

The essential requirements of a good rope climb are that the rope be strong enough and securely attached, that the supporting member be sturdy and steady, and that the rope be hung above a relatively soft and safe surface. It is best to use new rope. Manila rope is strong, and it has a fairly long life. Hemp and sisal have shorter fibers and shorter lives, and they should be checked regularly for wear or rot. Nylon rope is strong, but it tends to be too elastic, and its surface is slick and difficult to grip. One-inch thick manila rope is perfect. If you use 3/4-inch or narrower rope, it is best to use double or triple lengths. Knots can be tied every foot or every two feet, depending on how difficult you want the climb to be. Or, you can accept the ultimate challenge of climbing an unknotted rope.

Length ultimately depends on how high the suspension point is, but it is best to make the rope at least three feet longer than you think you can presently climb. Two of the benefits of rope climbing are learning determination in the form of a challenge, and discovering the mysterious ways of that force which athletes call second wind—the extra reserve of strength which we all have, and can learn to tap.

If you are using doubled or tripled lengths of rope, tie each individual length over the supporting member, so that if one breaks, another will prevent a fall.

The easiest and cheapest way to hang a rope is to suspend it from a sturdy tree limb. Avoid dry or rotten limbs. Select one which looks far stronger than you think you will need. It should branch out horizontally from the main trunk of a tree, but it should not droop down more than a few inches when your weight is on the rope. The rope should be at least three feet away from the tree trunk, allowing for a clear fall to the ground. Be sure there are no interfering limbs or spikes of broken limbs. Choose a limb which is above soft ground or turf, without any rocks, stumps, roots, or other dangerous protrusions. If possible, use the limb of a hardwood tree, such as oak or maple. Apple and cherry trees are also suitable, although they must be studied closely for dead and rotting limbs. Stay away from pine, spruce, aspen, and poplar, as they are soft-celled wood and tend to rot.

Be sure to knot the rope around the limb securely, but not so tightly that the loop will not move. Make a fairly loose loop. Double-tie all knots. For even more security, fasten the end of the rope to the shank by wrapping with strong baling wire.

An ideal loop would have a leather or metal sheath to minimize wear when the rope rubs against the limb.

Before attempting to climb the rope, test it from the ground with the full weight of *two* persons. The rope should thus be tested frequently, particularly in the spring after a hard winter. The loop at the top should also be examined regularly in order to find out if the movement of the rope on the limb has worn it through. If one strand of a three-strand rope breaks, remove the rope immediately and replace it with a new one, for the indications are that the fibers of the entire rope have broken down.

If there is not a good tree available, you can use one of the three methods of suspension suggested in figure 49. Diagram A represents a cantilevered suspension, made from used utility poles, which are often available at a telephone or electric company. Take the same care in examining and testing a utility pole as you would a tree limb, for used poles are often faulty. The ground end of the longer cantilevered post in diagram A should be secured firmly to the ground, either by wire ties across two deeply planted stakes, as shown, X, or by implantation in a block of poured concrete.

The A-frame suspension, shown in diagram B, can also be

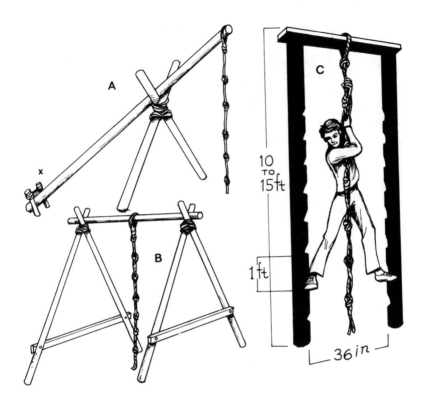

Figure 49

built from utility poles or it can be put together from heavy lumber (2-x-4-inch minimum, preferably 4-x-4-inch). Diagram C shows a vertical frame, made from peeled logs or utility poles, with a 2-x-6-inch lumber crossbar on top. The crossbar will be stronger if it is made from 4-x-4-inch lumber. If you use a two-by-six, make sure it has no large knots or other faults. The crossbar must be securely fastened to the tops of the poles, either with six-inch spikes or large bolts driven downward into the tops of the poles. The notches in the uprights can be cut with an axe or chain saw. Be careful to cut no deeper than one third of the pole's diameter. The step-ladder effect is an excellent way for beginning climbers to get a sense of progress while training their arm and shoulder muscles to take their entire body weights.

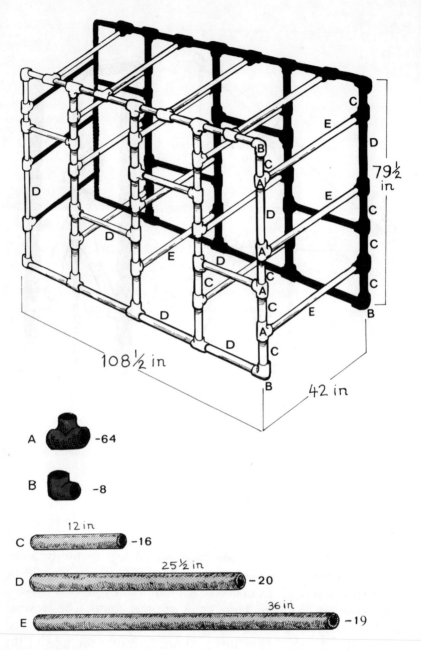

C

E

D

79½ in

B

C

A

D

C

A

E

D

D

C

E

A

C

A

C

E

D

C

A

C

D

B

108½ in

42 in

A ⬤ -64

B ⬤ -8

12 in

C ▬ -16

25½ in

D ▬ -20

36 in

E ▬ -19

Figure 50

B. Jungle Gym

This jungle gym, or set of monkey bars, is made from 1-inch (inside measurement) galvanized steel water pipe and fittings. Do not attempt to make it from plastic pipe because it will be too rickety. A more expensive version, using 1¼-inch pipe, can also be built. Because the larger pipe is stronger, you can extend the pipe length (E) figure 50, to fifty inches, and thus widen the structure.

The entire set of bars requires 127 parts, including all pipe lengths and fittings. At the bottom of figure 50 are diagrams showing the elbow and T-joints and the required number of each, as well as the three sizes of pipe, their lengths, and the required number of each. Letters indicate the positions of each pipe length and each type of fitting on one end of the structure. The same lengths and fittings are used, in an alternating pattern, throughout the structure.

You can cut and thread the pipe lengths yourself if you have tap and die tools. Or you can have the pieces cut and threaded at a plumbing supply house or a large hardware store. Used pipe and fittings are inexpensive and sometimes free. But you should be willing to spend the time and energy to locate them in a dump or a junkyard, take them apart, and cut and thread them to your requirements.

To assemble the structure, first put together the two longer side sections (running left to right in the illustration). When they are assembled, raise them and prop them into position with scrap lumber. Then fill in the cross members, E, turning them into place, one by one.

NOTE: Each of the cross members, E, must be cut at *one end only* with a *lefthand thread.* In this way, turning one end into place in one side section will simultaneously turn it into its socket in the opposite side section.

Finally, the jungle gym can be painted in a color or colors of your choice. Use a good outdoor enamel, and allow it to dry thoroughly before climbing aboard.

8.
SWINGING

A. Swings

Still the most popular method of "swinging" is, of course, to swing in an old-fashioned swing. Swings can be hung from tree branches. See page 66 for advice on selecting the right tree and branch. Find a horizontal limb that will hold the swing far enough away from the main tree trunk to allow it to swing freely. The swing can be suspended with rope, chain, or even cable. Use 3/4-inch Manila rope or a braided nylon rope that can take at least 300 pounds. The strength of chain depends on the quality of the steel and the method of linking. A welded link chain of light steel is safer than a bent link chain of thick metal. Galvanized, 3/16-inch steel cable comes with a protective vinyl coating, and is usually rated to carry 250 pounds. Most large hardware stores carry a selection of rope, chain, and cable.

Three varieties of swings are shown in figure 52. An old automobile tire makes the least expensive swing of all. However, it will tend to twist as it swings, so it is best suspended from heavy, braided rope, rather than from three-strand twisted rope. Diagram B shows the classic backyard swing, made from a twenty-six-inch length of 1-x-6-inch lumber. The swing is suspended from brackets of bent steel rod, threaded to take washers and nuts under the swing's seat. If you are using chain, the lengths can be secured to the seat brackets with special utility links, available at most hardware stores. If you are using cable, secure it with wire

71

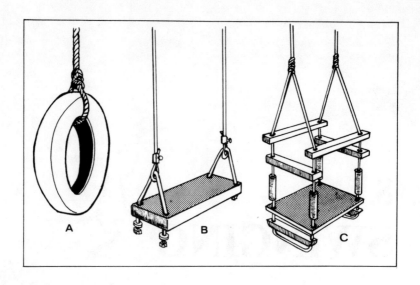

Figure 52

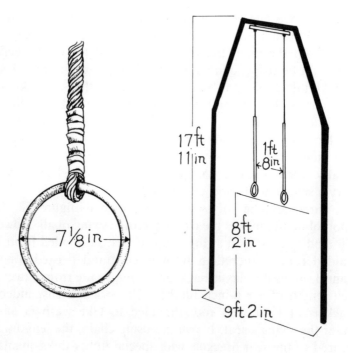

7⅛ in

17 ft
11 in

1 ft
8 in

8 ft
2 in

9 ft 2 in

Figure 53

rope clips, also sold in most hardware stores. Your hardware dealer can also provide you with appropriate hardware for the upper connections of chain or cable suspension.

Diagram C shows a small child's swing, which has safety bars at front and back to prevent its occupant from tumbling out. Cut the parts from 2-x-2-inch lumber and a 2-inch closet pole, drilled through the center to take the rope. String the entire assembly on strong nylon cord or on 1/4-inch steel cable. As you can see, the cord or cable will pass under the seat, with no knots or connections to wear loose.

B. Flying Rings

Figure 53 shows the official dimensions of a flying ring rig. The frame is a large and difficult project. It should be made from high quality steel, welded at the angles, and deeply imbedded in steel sleeves and concrete or affixed to the floor with metal plates and bolts. The utility pole A-frame structure, shown in figure 49, is clumsier looking but easier to build.

You can also suspend the rings from a tree limb, but try to keep the lengths and heights indicated in the drawing. The rings are best suspended from 1/4-inch or 1/2-inch galvanized steel cable. You may also use 1-inch Manila rope. The bottom length of the suspension cables (about forty inches) should be lightly padded and taped to prevent gymnasts from scraping their shoulders or thighs on the cable as they lift and spin.

Rings should be made of steel. (Do not cut rings from grained wood, as a break along the grain would be disastrous. The rings can be cut from very good plywood, at least one inch thick.) For steel or iron rings, find a small machine shop and ask if they will bend a 3/4-inch steel rod into a 6⅛-inch circle and weld it for you. It's not a difficult or a time-consuming job for a good metal worker, and the price might be acceptable. Afterward, polish the rings thoroughly with an electric polishing machine or polish them by hand with emery paper. Official rings are sometimes chromed for added smoothness, but a well polished steel ring is fine.

CAUTION: Performing gymnastics on flying rings can be dangerous, and requires proper training. Do not attempt any exercises beyond simple swinging and "skinning-the-cat" without the supervision of an informed adult or a professional gymnast.

C. Trapeze

Like swings and flying rings, a trapeze can be suspended from a stout tree limb or from an A-frame like that shown in figure 49. The safety factor is the first requirement of any trapeze.

The bar can be made of metal pipe, of solid steel rod, or of wood. If a softwood, such as pine or spruce, is used, it should have a straight grain and no cracks or splits. We strongly recommend the use of a hardwood, such as oak, maple, or ash. The best kind of wooden bar is cut from the handle of a shovel or a hoe which has undergone the test of time and wear; it should also have been smoothed to a high polish by use. The ideal diameter for a trapeze bar is given (A) in figure 54. Gymnasts with unusually large hands may prefer a bar 1½ inches in diameter.

Suspensions can be made of rope, chain, or cable; see page 71. Figure 54 shows a chain suspension, including the eye bolt and washers, used to attach the chain at the top. The eye bolt at the bottom should not be thicker than 3/8 inch. It goes through a hole drilled in the bar.

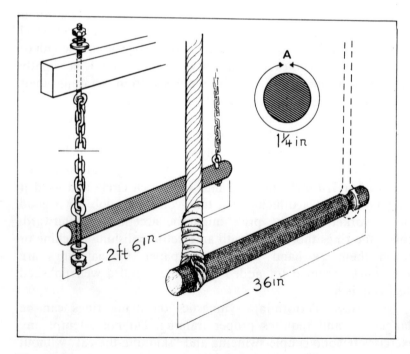

Figure 54

If you use cable, do not attempt to wrap or braid the loops at top and bottom. Instead, clamp them with wire rope nuts made for the purpose. These are available at large hardware stores. It is worth the expense to use the best hardware available. Even the best steel eventually suffers from a disintegrative ailment known as metal fatigue. A number of circus performers, gymnasts, and amateur athletes have been injured or killed because an eye bolt or rigging hook "crystallized" and broke as a result of prolonged use. Change all heavily used trapeze hardware once a year.

Make rope suspensions only from good Manila rope, 3/4 inch or 1 inch thick. See figure 54 for a rope suspension suitable for use only with a hardwood bar. The circular grooves at each end of the bar prevent the rope from slipping off. The grooves should not be cut any larger than a third of the bar's diameter, and they should be sanded as smooth as possible to minimize wear on the rope. Tightly wrap the joining point of the loop with wire, then cover the joint with at least two layers of strong surgical tape. Continue to wrap the joint to a point about twelve inches above the bar.

All trapezes should be frequently stress-tested with at least twice the weight they will be normally required to take.

Powdered resin helps sweaty hands to get a sure grip on the bar of a trapeze, a horizontal bar, or parallel bars. Powdered resin is available at large sporting goods stores. Finely ground blackboard chalk makes an acceptable substitute.

D. Hand-Over-Hand Ladder

Swinging from an overhead ladder, and going hand-over-hand from rung to rung, builds up shoulder and arm muscles. The ladder, shown in figure 55, can be mounted by itself or it can be part of constructions, such as the target wall, figure 8; the kiddie kube, figure 74; and the sports wall, figures 76 and 77.

The rungs should be set into runners of 2-x-6-inch lumber or very good, clear 2-x-4-inch lumber. The rungs themselves can be made from a 1¼-inch pine closet pole of a good clear grain, but they are best made from hardwood. Drill holes in the lumber, and apply epoxy or white glue to the holes and rungs. Insert the rungs, and secure them with nails or screws driven through the 2-x-6-inch runners and into both ends of each rung, as shown, A.

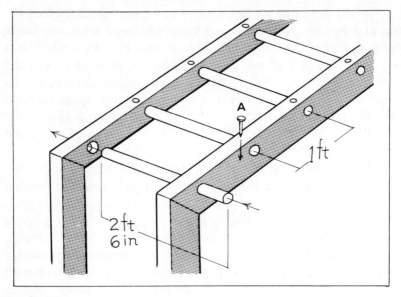

Figure 55

E. Hand-Over-Hand Spool

The rolling, hand-over-hand spool is made from a large wooden spool of the sort used for heavy electric cable. Such spools can usually be obtained for a modest price from a telephone company. Ask the company's customer service department to connect you with the warehouse, and try to talk directly to the warehouse manager. You might make a small contribution in exchange for a used spool or two. Or, if you know the location of a telephone service center and warehouse, you might try approaching the manager directly. If possible, select a spool that has not been too badly weathered. By placing it on its flat side and pushing your weight against it, you can discover if it is too rickety for use. It should not wobble, and the wood along the rim and around the tie bolts should not be spongy or rotten.

The illustration at the bottom of figure 56 shows a spool that is forty-one inches in diameter. Since there are larger and smaller spools, adjust the length of the rungs to fit the measurements of your particular spool.

Rungs should be at least 1¼ inches in diameter. You can use straight-grained, pine closet pole, but hardwood is best. First drill the holes at regular intervals around the rim, then insert the rungs

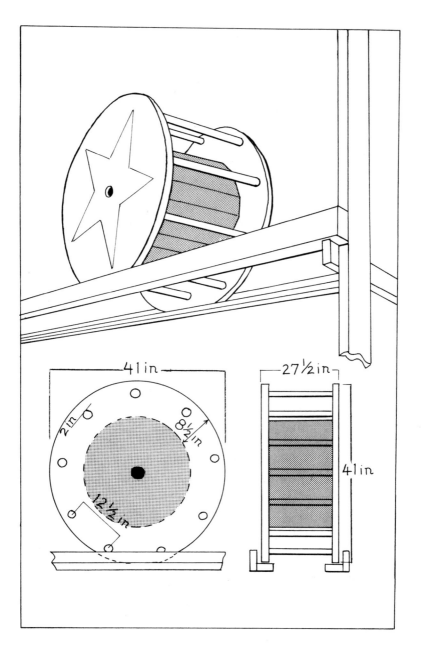

Figure 56

according to the directions for the ladder, page 75. Secure them with plenty of glue, and drive nails or screws through the rim and into both ends of each rung.

The spool can then be mounted on a double track of 2-x-4-inch or 2-x-6-inch lumber, as suggested at the top of figure 56. This track can be set up on top of a simple target wall, see page 8, or as a part of the more complex sports wall described in chapter 11, section D.

F. Horizontal Bar

A sturdy horizontal bar requires upright posts, which are rigidly supported and will not wobble or sway. Posts can be made of 2-inch pipe in the same manner as the women's asymmetrical bars, described on page 82. Wooden posts should be made from 4-x-4-inch lumber. They can be rooted in a poured concrete block or in a cement block filled with poured concrete, as indicated in diagram A, figure 57. Each post should extend at least two feet (preferably three feet) below ground level. Paint a few feet of the bottom of the posts with creosote to prolong life. A good concrete foundation will usually keep the posts rigidly upright, but if there is still too much movement, brace each post on either side with lengths of 2-x-4-inch lumber or with guy wires, see H, figure 57.

The bar itself should be made of 1¼-inch steel pipe or a solid steel rod. Diagram B shows the means of fitting the ends of the bar into holes drilled, across grain, into the upright posts. For a pipe bar, cut the main length 7 feet, 6 inches long, then cut two smaller lengths 3½ inches long. Drill holes into these shorter lengths for later insertion, as per C, upper right corner of figure 57.

The pipe is secured in each hole by use of two pipe fittings, D and F, called a straight joint and an end plug, respectively. First screw the straight joint, D, into place on the end of the longer length. Then screw the short pipe length, E, into D. Insert E into the hole in the post, pushing it through until fitting D acts as a snug collar against the post. Then screw the end plug, F, onto the end of the short length, E. Tighten all fittings to make sure the pipe will not move to the left or right. Finally, insert a pin of 3/8-inch tie rod, through a hole drilled downward from the top of the post, and into the hole in the short length, E. This will keep the bar from rolling in the gymnast's hands.

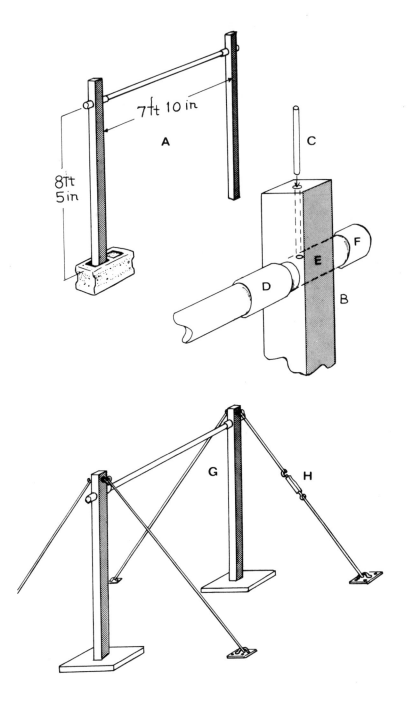

7 ft 10 in

A

8 ft 5 in

C

E

D

F

B

G

H

Figure 57

An indoor horizontal bar can be constructed from wood, pipe, and steel cable, as indicated (G) in figure 57. Each post has a footing base of 1-inch plywood, as shown. Add 2-x-4-inch angle braces for extra strength, as illustrated in figure 30. The bar is secured with fittings and pin, as indicated for the outdoor version, A through F, figure 57. Each post has a footing base of 1-inch plywood, as shown. Add 2-x-4-inch angle braces for extra strength, as shown in figure 30. The bar is secured with footings and a pin, as indicated for the outdoor version, A through F.

The guy wires are made from 3/16-inch galvanized steel cable, secured at the tops of the posts with eye bolts, and at the bottoms to steel plates screwed or bolted to the floor. In order to adjust cable tension, insert turnbuckles, as indicated, H.

G. Parallel Bars

A set of parallel bars should have a rigid and solidly placed base, and strong but supple bars.

Diagram B, figure 58, shows a professional set of indoor bars. Diagram A gives the proper dimensions and shows a frame for an outdoor set of bars. The frame is made of 1½-inch pipe, with the bottoms of the legs set in poured concrete or in cement blocks. The tops end in T-joints. Each of the two parallel bars consists of three pieces of 1½-inch pipe, one long and two short. The pipes are threaded so that they can be screwed into the T-joints and form one continuous bar. Or, the T-joints can be reamed out to take a pair of continuous wooden bars. Wooden bars should be of the diameter shown, D, and be made of well-seasoned hardwood, such as maple or ash.

Such a set of parallel bars will not be strictly official, since the parallel bars should run straight, and be without any joints to interfere with the gymnast's hands. The conventional method of arranging this is suggested in diagrams B and C, where the upright makes a slight jog inward and is inserted *into* the bar. This can be done with a set of solid steel or pipe bars as well, but it requires welding equipment.

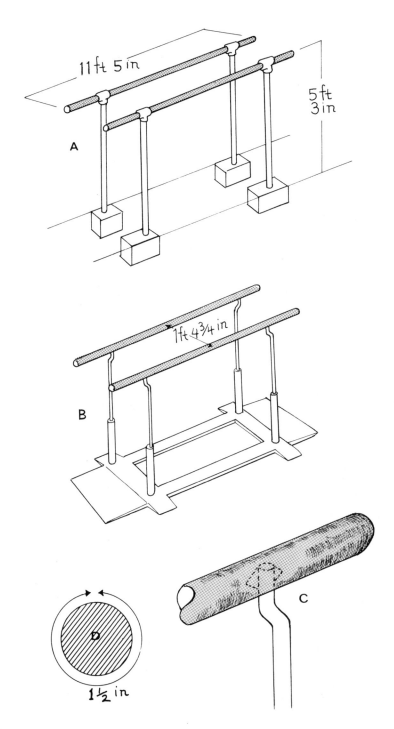

Figure 58

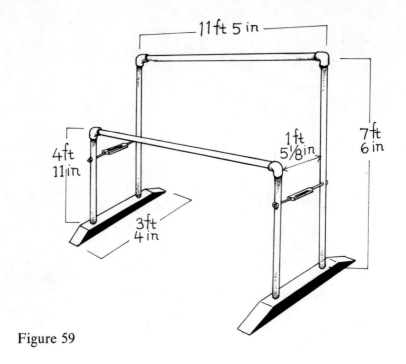

Figure 59

H. Women's Asymmetrical Bars

It's difficult to make this apparatus correctly in a home workshop, because the frame and bars must be sturdy enough to hold together, yet supple enough (with enough "whip" in the bars) to assist the gymnast in her swings and spins. This project requires special steel and fittings.

However, a crude backyard or basement version can be constructed by following the dimensions given in figure 59, and the instructions already offered in various similar pieces of equipment, such as the trapeze, the horizontal bar, and the parallel bars.

Make the bars and framework from 1¼-inch galvanized steel water pipe and fittings. The baseboards should be made of heavy lumber, preferably 4-x-4-inch or larger. The legs of an outdoor version must be firmly and deeply rooted in poured concrete or in cement blocks filled with concrete.

Note the turnbuckles between the uprights of the low and high bars. These enable adjustments to be made in the area between the opposite uprights.

9.
BALANCING

A. Balance Beam

The ideal balance beam should be straight and smooth-surfaced, and mounted on sturdy and unshakable legs. The beam should have unobstructed top and side surfaces, so that the gymnast will not trip while performing.

Official beams measure four inches across the top surface, and are six inches deep. Our beam, figure 61, uses the easier-to-come by 4-x-4-inch lumber. Although the depth is less, the more important top surface width meets the official requirement of four inches.

The legs, cross braces, and angle braces of the frame can be made from 2-x-4-inch lumber, but 2-x-6-inch is even better. The upper junction of each pair of legs is secured with a triangular plate of 1-inch plywood, as shown in diagram C and the dotted lines of D. The plate is held in place with flatheaded screws. The juncture of angle brace and cross brace is shown in the inset circle, B. Secure the beam to the leg assemblies by first drilling holes to take 3/8-x-6-inch lag bolts, then countersink the holes to a 3/4-inch depth. Once the lag bolts are screwed down through the beam and into the leg assemblies, the bolt heads will be well below the top surface of the beam. The bolt heads and countersink holes can then be covered with plastic wood putty to even the surface of the beam. Two applications of putty will be required, since the first will sink a bit.

Finally, the beam must be well sanded, particularly along the top surface and edges. There should not be any rough spots or splinters to snag the gymnast's feet.

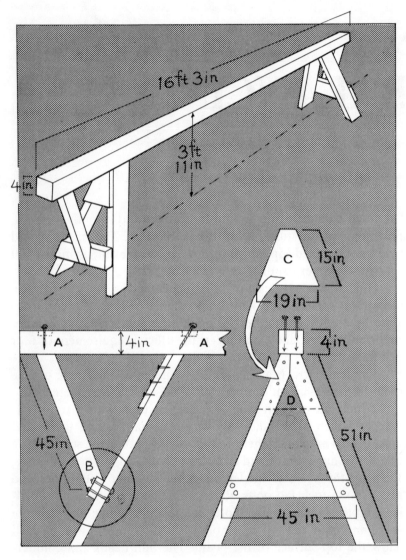

Figure 61

B. Teeter-Totter

This age-old balance-and-counterbalance apparatus, which can be made quickly and inexpensively, will provide hours of exercise and fun, particularly for younger athletes.

The plank should be fashioned from a good grade of straight-grained wood, preferably 2-x-12-inch lumber. A common length is twelve feet. The plank can be cut with crescent indentations to accommodate the teeter-totterer's knees, as shown in diagram A, figure 62. Handles, just in front of the seat, can be added for extra security. Large, metal drawer handles are the least costly and the easiest to install. You can add strips of 1-x-4-inch lumber, nailed to the underside of the plank, to create a slot for the support cross bar. The strips will keep the plank from wheeling or sliding out of position.

The revolving teeter-totter, suggested in diagram B, has a hole in the center of the plank which allows the plank to swivel

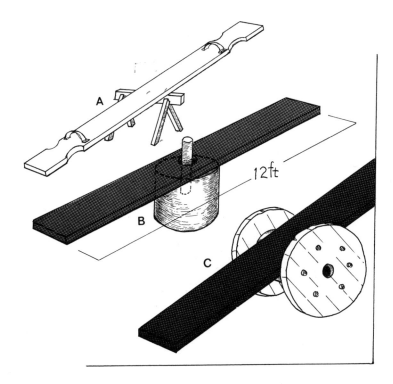

Figure 62

atop a pedestal. Make the pedestal from a two- or three-foot length of sawed log. Drill a six-inch hole in the top of the log and insert a length of tree limb or other round lumber no less than three inches in diameter.

Diagram C shows a teeter-totter with a cable spool for a pedestal. See chapter 8, section E for information on how to acquire such a spool.

C. Log Roll

Log rolling is another good way to develop balance and body grace. Start by standing on a length of peeled or rough log. Try to roll it forward and backward. The log should be at least twelve inches in diameter (preferably larger) and three or more feet long.

Figure 63 shows a log mounted on a heavy steel rod and supported by two upright posts. Dimensions depend on the size of the logs. Used utility poles can be substituted, see page 66.

3ft

4ft

Figure 63

The hardware for this apparatus will not be easy to come by, but a large junkyard or auto wrecking establishment should have some heavy steel rod. The rod must be threaded to take bolts and washers. You will need two rods, one for each end of the log. They should be set as deeply as possible into the ends of the log, but the longest of commonly available drills will limit the depth to six or eight inches. Therefore, the ends of the log should be as snug as possible against the sides of the uprights, leaving only enough tolerance for several washers and sufficient clearance for the log to turn easily. The ends of the rolling log should be squared, or as close to perpendicular to the length, as possible.

Log rolling may also be practiced on the inside circumference of a cable spool set sideways on its rims. See chapter 8, section E for tips on acquiring a cable spool.

10. LIFTING

A. Barbells

The bar should be strong enough to take the weight without bowing, and the disks should be of a consistent weight and should not turn on the bar during lifting.

A homemade set of barbells is shown in figure 65. The bar is five feet, eight inches in length, made of 1¼-inch steel water pipe or solid rod. Each end of the bar is designed so that a flange in the socket of each weight disk slides into a four-inch slot in the bar. This will keep the disk from turning on the bar when the bar is lifted. For a pipe bar, three pieces are needed for each end, as shown, middle of figure 65. A six-inch length of pipe, C, is threaded on both ends, and cut with the slot, four inches long and 3/8 inch wide. The body of the pipe, A, is screwed into a straight joint, B. B will act as a collar to keep the weight from sliding inward along the bar. B is then screwed onto C. The weight disk is then slipped over C, and its flange is fitted into the slot. Finally, an end cap, D, is screwed onto the assembly until it rests tightly against the weight disk. This acts as a second collar to help hold the weight in place. The opposite end of the bar should have the same arrangement of A, B, C, and D.

The arrangement shown allows for two three-inch disks to be mounted. If only one disk weight is used, the slack area between the disk and the end cap can be shimmed with a number of large

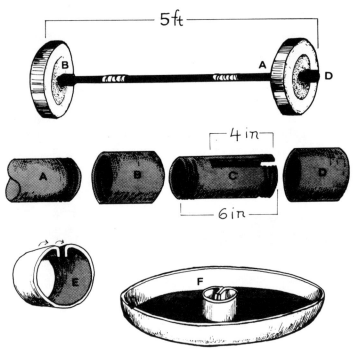

Figure 65

washers or with a single washerlike shim made from three disks of 1-inch plywood. They should be cut like washers and glued face to face.

The disk weights, or "bells," are made of cement poured into suitable molds—cake pans, cheese boxes, cookie canisters or any other disk-shaped receptacle. We used plastic flying saucers (Frisbees).

Prepare your mold as indicated, F, first cutting a 1¼-inch hole in the center. Next, fashion from sheet metal a core representing the socket, as indicated, F. Set this core upright in the hole in the center of the mold. Now mix up a batch of premixed concrete, masonry mix, or any other fine-sand mix. You can prepare enough for one disk at a time or you can do several disks at once. Pour the mix into the mold, making sure that there are no bubbles and that the mix settles snugly around the core. Allow the mix to dry thoroughly for seventy-two hours, but dampen it occasionally to prevent it from cracking. Such a disk, made from a standard-size Frisbee, will weigh approximately four pounds. To finish, cut a 1/4-inch plywood or plastic disk the same size as the mold, and lay it over the exposed cement face. Tape the entire disk thoroughly with plastic electrician's tape.

To make an eight-pound weight, use two Frisbees. Pour each separately, then tape two together.

It should now be possible to mount the disks on the bar. Follow the procedure indicated above: A, B, C, and D.

It is advisable and officially permissible to add hand grips to the bar, as shown at the top of figure 65. These can be made of rubber hose of the right diameter to fit tightly on the bar. Or you can wrap the gripping areas with a double layer of surgical or electrician's tape.

B. Exercise Bench

An exercise bench, such as the one shown in figure 66, is useful for weight lifting and for general body building. The body builder can do exercises or lift weights while seated or lying prone. The table is even useful for an occasional, but necessary rest. Our table folds down at one end to form an incline for situps and/or lifting. The posts at the table's opposite end can be notched to hold barbells, as shown. The barbells can be lifted from this position, or they can anchor a lifter's ankles, as demonstrated at the top of the illustration. Wing nuts on the bolts holding each leg can be tightened to hold the leg in an up or down position. (CAUTION: Never position barbells on the notched posts until you are certain that the wing nuts are tight enough to keep the posts from folding under. Use lock washers under each wing nut.)

Cut the bench top in the dimensions shown from 3/4-inch or 1-inch interior plywood. Add a padding of one inch of foam. Cover this with heavy vinyl, and tack the covering around the underside of the bench top. The top should be secured to the frame with 3-inch flatheaded wood screws.

Make the frame from 2-x-6-inch lumber and the legs from 2-x-4-inch lumber, cut in the dimensions shown. Each set of legs is held together by a cross bar of either 2-x-2-inch or 1-x-4-inch lumber. The crossbar can be glued and nailed or, better yet, sunk into squared sockets in each leg, as indicated, C. 1/4-x-4-inch flatheaded screws or lag bolts hold the frame together, B. The legs are held by 3/8-x-6-inch stove bolts, A. Each bolt should be installed, along with one smooth washer on each side, one lock washer on the inside, and one wing nut for tightening.

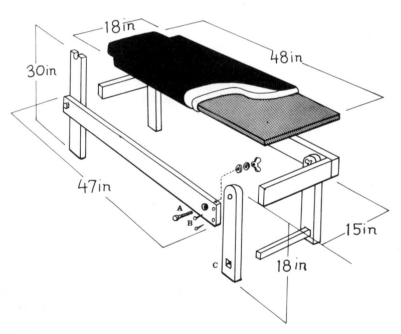

Figure 66

C. Wall Weights

Here is an old, but inexpensive and useful isometric device that helps the conditioning of a variety of muscles. You can face the apparatus when pulling the weights. Or you can turn your back to it or lie down and pull the weights with either your hands or your feet. The device can be put together in a few hours with assorted "found" hardware. Dimensions will depend on what size weights or sand containers you use.

As you can see in figure 67, the apparatus consists of two sets of weights, connected to cords or cables which pass over pulleys. The pulleys are attached to the walls, and from there to handles held in the hands or hooked over the feet. For the pull cables, use braided nylon rope or 1/8-inch steel galvanized cable. Both are available at large hardware stores. Avoid twisted rope because it can unravel and foul the pulleys. Clothesline pulleys or any small sheave pulleys are suitable. They are attached to U-bolts which in turn are attached to a wooden block. The block is bolted or screwed to a wall.

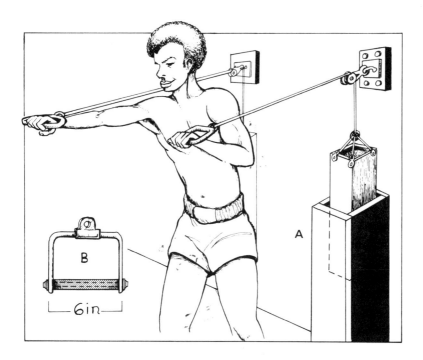

Figure 67

The counterweights can be actual weights, such as window-sash weights, or they can be boxes filled with gravel or sand. The advantage of the filled boxes is that the weight can be increased or decreased by adjusting the contents. Weights should be controlled by some kind of track or sleeve to keep them from swinging and banging against the wall. The long box indicated, A, figure 67, is an old cracker tin. A similar box might be made by cutting the top off of a kerosene or other large metal container. Or it can be made from sheet metal, cold-riveted at the seams. The sleeve or guide box shown can be made from 1-x-10-inch lumber in dimensions that will allow the weight box to slide easily up and down, but prevent it from swinging. This guide box is fastened to the wall with bolts or molly screws. Adjust the dimensions of our guide box or tracks to accommodate your particular weights or weight box. The box is slung from a truss, composed of short lengths of rope or wire, and gathered into a single, steel key ring. Any similar truss arrangement will be suitable, as long as it pulls the box directly upward toward the pulley.

We made our handles from a toilet paper dispenser of the sort sold in hardware and household supply stores. The hand grip, made from a collapsible tube, is designed for easy removal. To make sure it stayed in place, we ran a stove bolt through it, as shown, B. Any other stirruplike piece of hardware can be used. Or you can make one with a piece of doweling (for the hand grip) and a steel strap, bent to form the stirrup.

11.
COMBOS

A. Indoor Layout

The various devices described in this book can be assembled to make a gymnasium suited to your particular needs. Figures 69, 70, and 71 show the floor plans for three combination gyms. Figure 69 is a plan for a gym that is mostly devoted to combat sports and body building. It accommodates the following pieces of equipment:

    a. Speed Bag Platform, chapter 3, section C.
    b. Boxing and Wrestling Ring, chapter 3, section D.
    c. Tumbling and Exercise Mat, chapter 3, section E.
    d. Barbells, chapter 10, section A.
    e. Wall Weights, chapter 10, section C.
    f. Exercise Bench, chapter 10, section B.

Figure 70 presupposes the use of a very large room. It shows a gym mostly devoted to gymnastics. It accommodates the following pieces of equipment; the first two can be stored near one wall, when not in use.

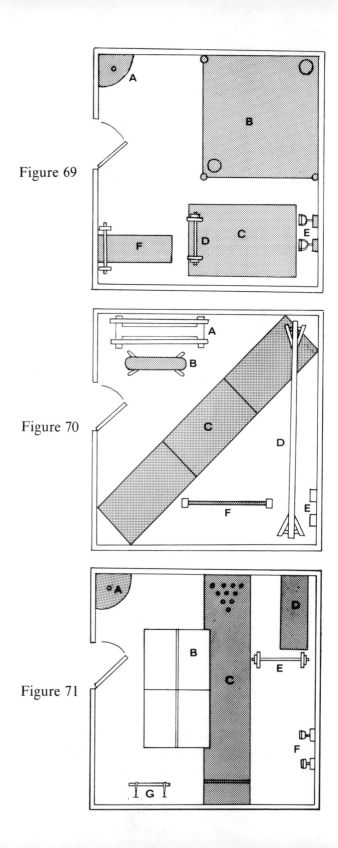

Figure 69

Figure 70

Figure 71

a. Parallel Bars, chapter 8, section G.
b. Vaulting Horse, chapter 6, section B.
c. Tumbling Mats, chapter 3, section E.
d. Balance Beam, chapter 9, section A.
e. Wall Weights, chapter 10, section C.
f. Horizontal Bar, chapter 8, section F.

Figure 71 shows a layout for a general family gym. It can be constructed in a moderately large basement, with a sufficient amount of overhead clearance and overhead beams for the installation of a trapeze. The table tennis table can be dismantled and moved aside when the small bowling alley is being used. This gym accommodates the following equipment:

a. Speed Bag, chapter 3, section C.
b. Table Tennis Table, chapter 2, section G.
c. Bowling Alley, chapter 1, section G.
d. Exercise Table, chapter 10, section B.
e. Barbells, chapter 10, section A.
f. Wall Weights, chapter 10, section C.
g. Trapeze, chapter 8, section C.

Your own combination layout must, of course, be adjusted to fit the dimensions of the available area. First take complete measurements of the room, basement, or garage you plan to use. But don't fail to take into consideration the locations of doors and windows and whether they open inward or outward. Ceiling height is another important consideration, especially for such devices as the horizontal bar, which requires overhead clearance almost equal to the height of the apparatus itself. You must remember, also, that some pieces of apparatus can be moved aside when not in use, while others are attached more or less permanently in place.

B. Outdoor Layout

Although there is usually much more room available for an outdoor combination gym, it should first be carefully planned on paper. If it's likely that more than one piece of apparatus will be in use at any one time, be sure that the lines of action won't cross and cause athletes to collide or interfere with one another. Figure 72 illustrates only one of the many possible combinations of equipment:

a. Auto Tire High Step, chapter 4, section B.
b. Target Wall with Overhead Ladder, chapter 1, section C; chapter 8, section D.
c. High Jump, chapter 5, section C.
d. Horizontal Bar, chapter 8, section F.
e. Basketball Backboard, chapter 1, section A, Garage-Mounted.
f. Balance Beam, chapter 8, section A.
g. Running Track, chapter 4, section D.
h. Hurdles, chapter 5, section A.
i. Finishing Posts, chapter 4, section E.
j. Swing, chapter 8, section A.

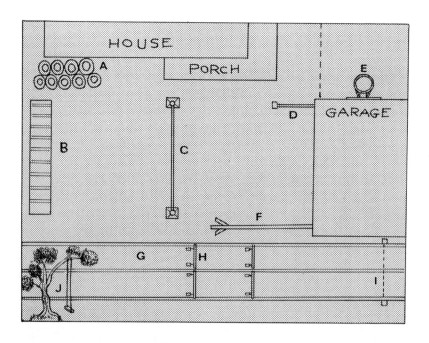

Figure 72

C. Kiddie Kube

It is also possible to combine various kinds of exercise and play apparatus into a single construction. Figures 73 and 74 illustrate a kiddie kube. This is designed as a single construction

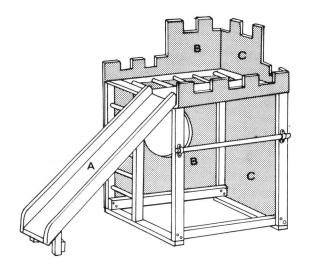

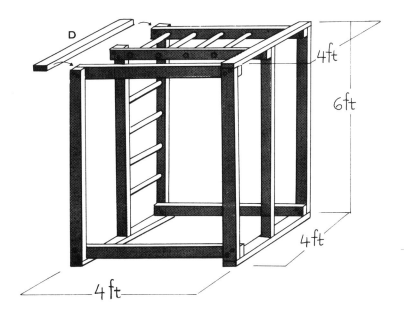

Figure 73

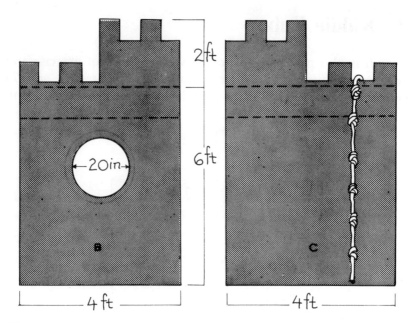

Figure 74

for young children. It is made of readily available lumber and hardware, and it can be put together over a weekend.

The frame is constructed as indicated at the bottom of figure 73. Use 2-x-4-inch lumber for all posts and stringers, including the cross brace, D. Construct the vertical and overhead ladders according to the directions given on page 75. Put the main parts of the frame together with 3/8-x-4-inch lag bolts.

Once the frame is assembled, cut the two side panels from two sheets of 3/8-inch exterior plywood, according to the dimensions in figure 74. The round hole in panel B is a target hole for football passing. It can also be cut in a dimension suitable for a baseball-pitching target, see page 10. Or the wall can be painted with another target or rebound pattern, see page 10. In addition, a larger hole can be cut, as indicated B, figure 73, to form a round portal for peeking and for climbing in and out.

Once the panels are cut, sand them to remove any splinters. Then attach the panels to the frame with 2-inch flatheaded screws, as shown in figure 73.

A slide can be added, as shown in figure 73. The bottom panel of the slide can be made from 1-x-12-inch shelving lumber or it can be cut from 1-inch plywood. The sides of the chute

100

should be made with 1-x-6-inch lumber. Attach the sides to the bottom panel with 2-inch flatheaded screws. Screw them from the bottom up, first through the panel, then into the side panels. For a smooth and splinterless slide, thoroughly sand the panels. The surface should then be painted with several coats of exterior enamel or marine varnish. They can also be sprayed with several coats of liquid acrylic, and finished with paste wax. Or you can line the chute with tin or aluminum sheeting, making sure that there are no rough seams that might harm the slider. Use nails and tacks only on the underside of the slide.

Paint the kube if you wish. A painted stone effect, appropriate for its play castle appearance, can be achieved by first painting the panels gray. Allow the paint to dry, then outline the shapes of stones with narrow white lines.

D. Sports Wall

Here is a complicated construction requiring nearly a week of work to complete. However, it can be built with common lumber and hardware to accommodate a variety of devices on a single, main frame. The side with the open back serves as a goal for football, soccer, and other ball sports, see page 31. On the top, a hand-over-hand spool rolls on rails, see page 76. A basketball backboard is attached at one end, see page 1. At the opposite end is a climbing ladder, see page 75, with a speed bag platform attached, see page 38. The front side can be used for a number of purposes. Figure 75 shows a climbing rope (page 65) and a target panel with a baseball pitching hole (page 10). Other target or rebound panels described on pages 8 and 24, can be added.

The frame can be built entirely from 2-x-4-inch lumber. Take great care in selecting lumber that is straight, long grained, and without knots or faults. The four lengths that make up the top rails *must* be straight and strong, for they carry the weight of the spool. You may want to use 2-x-6-inch lumber for the overhead rails and the four corner posts; this will provide added stability to the whole structure, and provide a wider track for the spool.

First build the end trusses, as shown, B, figure 76. The cross ties are attached to the uprights on the *inside,* with 3/8-x-6-inch stove bolts and lock washers. These bolts also secure the angle braces, which form an **X** in the middle of the truss. These can be

101

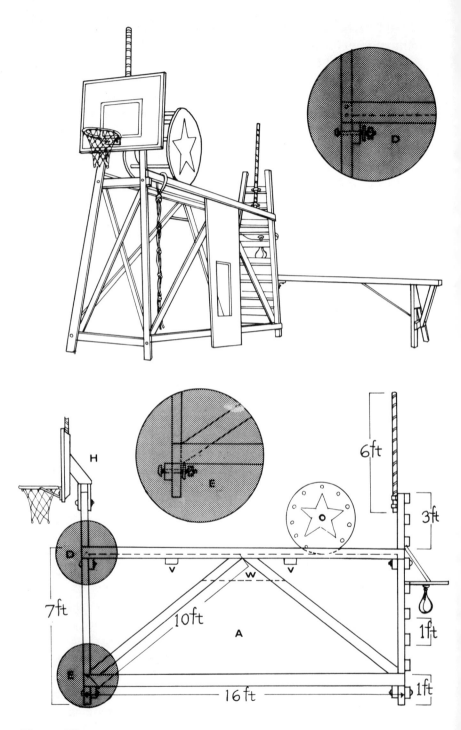

Figure 75

made from 1-x-4-inch lumber. Notice that the cross ties at both top and bottom extend an inch on each side, as shown in inserts F and G, figure 76. These extensions will support the overhead rails on top and the long stringers below. The same is true of both end trusses, although one of them does not form an **X**. Instead, it is reinforced with ladder rungs of 2-x-4-inch lumber, cut to fit and spaced at twelve-inch intervals along the full height of the truss. For safety, secure each rung with 5-inch stove bolts, lock washers, and nuts.

The basketball backboard and speed-bag platform should not be added until the entire frame has been assembled.

Once the end trusses are ready, get together the lumber for the rails and bottom stringers. This material includes the four lengths of 2-x-4-inch (or 2-x-6-inch) lumber for the rails, as well as the two stringers, one for each side. Each of the six pieces should be sixteen feet long, as shown in figure 75, A, and figure 76, G.

You will need help to assemble the frame. Raise one end truss and hold or prop it upright. Then raise the other end truss about sixteen feet. Now, climb a step ladder and lift one end of the long side pieces of rail into position. Attach it as shown, X, in inset F, figure 76, in inset D, figure 75. Secure it with 4-inch spikes, driven halfway in. Next, do the same with the other side rail. Your two end frames are now connected along the top, enabling you to make adjustments in the ground positions of the end trusses. Making sure that the structure is braced by your helpers, adjust the trusses so that they are perpendicular to the ground and squarely opposite one another. Once they are set, you may add the bottom stringers. Drive in spikes just deep enough to hold the stringers in place. At the bottom of diagram B, figure 76, you'll note that the front stringer is 8½ inches above the ground, while the rear stringer runs along the ground surface. The reason for this is to allow the goal side of the wall to remain relatively unobstructed.

Check the structure again to make sure that the end trusses are vertical and squarely facing one another, and that the side rails and bottom stringers are in proper alignment. Then secure them permanently by either driving in the spikes and adding others or by removing the spikes, one by one, and substituting 3/8-x-5-inch lag bolts, as shown in inset G, figure 76.

The basic frame is now secured, and it should hold in place while you add the angle braces and the two sixteen-foot lengths which form the bottom of the spool rail.

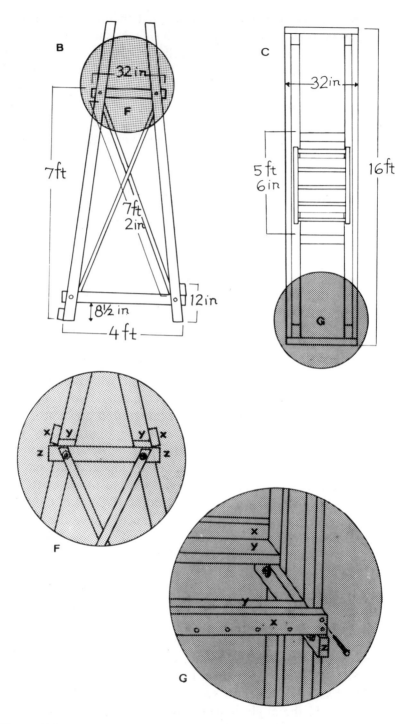

B

32 in

F

7ft

7ft
2in

8½ in

12in

4 ft

C

32in

5 ft
6in

16ft

G

F

x y y x
z z

G

x
y

y

o x o

z

Figure 76

104

Lay each rail length beside its side rail, resting it on the upper edge of the end truss's cross tie, as shown, Y, in insets F and G, figure 76; and X, inset D, figure 75. Secure the ends of each rail to the end of each cross tie with 4-inch spikes or 3/8-x-3-inch lag bolts. If you have taken care to use straight lumber, the bottom rail should now fit snugly beside its companion side rail. The side rail will tilt at a slight angle due to the tapered design of the end trusses, but it can still be attached to the bottom rail. Drive 4-inch spikes or 3/8-x-4-inch lag bolts through the side rail and into the side edge of the bottom rail at intervals of no less than eight inches, as indicated by the open dots along the side rail in inset G, figure 76. It is vital that the two rails be securely attached so that the side rail will not spread away from the bottom rail and allow the spool to slip down.

Next, place the angle braces, as shown in diagram A, figure 75 (they form the inverted V of the side profile). There are four braces, two to each side. They join the bottom of each end truss, as shown in inset E, figure 75, and rest on the upper edge of the cross tie. The weight of the spool will hold them firmly in place, but they should also be attached with 4-inch spikes.

Each pair of angle braces meets at the center of the upper railing, where they must be positioned so that the butt end (cut at an angle) helps support the bottom rail of the spool track. This means that the upper end of each brace should be positioned exactly in the center of the bottom surface of the rail. Fasten them with 4-inch spikes or 3-inch lag bolts, driven downward through the rail and into the end grain of the angle brace. Finally, reinforce the top of the inverted V with a triangular plate cut from 1/2-inch or 5/8-inch plywood, as indicated, W, in diagram A, figure 75.

The main structure is now almost complete. Climb the laddered end truss, and heave your weight back and forth cautiously to make sure all connections are secure. Test the long spool railings to see if they tend to spread apart from one another toward their centers. Use a tape measure to see if the distance between the rails is exactly the same for the full length of the spool track. If the rails spread more than two inches at any point along their length, you should add cross ties of 2-x-4-inch lumber, as indicated, V, diagram A, figure 75. Although these extra cross ties will interfere to some degree with the use of the hand-over-hand spool, they will prevent the rails from spreading and the spool from falling.

The hand-over-hand spool is made from a discarded telephone cable spool, as described on page 76. It should now be raised onto the rails. This will require the help of two strong persons. The spool can be rolled up a makeshift ramp with the help of a rope or a block-and-tackle. We raised it by hand from the bed of a pickup truck, parked beside the sports wall.

Before attempting to swing from the rungs of the spool, stand on a raised plank or on one of the bottom stringers. Cautiously roll the spool the full length of the rails and then back again. The side rails should keep it on track. If the rails spread so that more than a quarter of an inch of the rolling edge of the spool extends over the inside edge of the rail, then you must add the railing cross ties previously mentioned. If your railing lumber is straight, this should not happen.

You are now ready to start adding the other equipment. The basketball backboard can be bolted directly to the uprights of the open-end truss, but this will not raise the basket to the official height of ten feet from the playing surface. See page 00 for suggestions on the proper mounting of a backboard so that the board is held well away from the uprights. For the best results, devise an angle truss like the one suggested, H, figure 75. Design it so that it will raise the basket to the required ten feet. The truss can be made from lumber and bent iron strapping, bolted to the tops of the truss uprights, as suggested, H, figure 75.

Mount the punching bag platform (see chapter 3, section C) on the opposite end truss, as shown in diagram A, figure 75.

For the striped goal posts on each end truss, cut six- or eight-foot lengths of 1-inch CPVC plastic water pipe. Wrap each length with plastic electrician's tape for the striped effect, then fix it in place with common pipe brackets, available at most hardware stores.

For a rope climb, see chapter 7, section A.

Add one, two, or three target panels (see page 8) on the front side. Tack them along the top and bottom with nails if you intend to disassemble them. Attach them with 2-inch flatheaded screws if they are to be permanent. You can also install three uncut panels and paint them with a tennis net line, see page 24.

Other pieces of apparatus may be added by using the sports wall for partial support. Our drawing, top of figure 75, shows a balance beam extending from the side of the ladder truss. See page 83 for balance beam dimensions and construction. A horizontal bar (page 78) might be substituted for the balance beam, or added to another corner of the structure. A small trapeze can be hung from the rails, see chapter 8, section C.

Paint the structure whatever color you wish. Blue looks nice against a green lawn. A yellow star, painted on both sides of the spool, gives a circus air to your sports wall.

Now it's time to think about what you have learned. Build with care, enjoy what you have built, play with spirit, and exercise for health.

BOOKS FOR FURTHER READING

Babbitt, Diane. *Gymnastic Apparatus Exercises for Girls.* New York: Ronald Press, 1964.

Conger, Ray, *Track and Field.* New York: Ronald Press, 1938.

Diagram Visual Information Ltd. (The Diagram Group). *Rules of the Game: The Complete Illustrated Encyclopedia of All the Sports of the World.* New York: Paddington Press, 1974.

Horis, Ford (ed.) *The Sports Encyclopedia.* New York: Praeger, 1976.

Jennison, Keith (ed.). *The Concise Encyclopedia of Sports.* New York: Franklin Watts, 1970.

Maddox, Gordon T. *Men's Gymnastics.* Pacific Palisades, Calif.: Goodyear, 1970.

Pratt, John and Benagh, Jim. *The Official Encyclopedia of Sports.* New York: Franklin Watts, 1964.

Ryan, Frank. *Gymnastics for Girls.* New York: Viking Press, 1976.

Webster's Sports Dictionary. Springfield, Mass.: Merriam, 1976.

COMMON METRIC EQUIVALENTS
AND CONVERSIONS

Approximate

1 inch	= 25 millimeters
1 foot	= 0.3 meter
1 yard	= 0.9 meter
1 square inch	= 6.5 square centimeters
1 square foot	= 0.09 square meter
1 square yard	= 0.8 square meter
1 millimeter	= 0.04 inch
1 meter	= 3.3 feet
1 meter	= 1.1 yards
1 square centimeter	= 0.16 square inch

Accurate to Parts Per Million

inches × 25.4	= millimeters
feet × 0.3048	= meters
yards × 0.9144	= meters
square inches × 6.4516	= square centimeters
square feet × 0.092903	= square meters
square yards × 0.836127	= square meters

INDEX

Ladder, hand-over-hand, 75
Landing pads, 55
Log roll, 87
Long jump, 53

Martial arts mats, 41
Mats
    boxing, 39
    tumbling, 41
    wrestling, 41

Netball, woman's, 1
Nets
    badminton, 25
    basketball, 1
    rebound, 12
    service, 25
    tennis, 25

Olympics, x, 1
Olympic hurdles, 51
Outdoor gym layouts, 98

Paddle-ball, 24
Parallel bars, 80
Pentathalon hurdle, 51
Pin, bowling, 17
Ping-pong table, 29
Pipe, basketball backboard, 6
Piste, fencing, 44
Pitching, baseball, 23
Pole vault, 57
Pommel horse, 57
Punching bag, 38
Putting cup, 28

Rebound net, 12
Rebound wall, 24
Relay baton, 47
Ring, boxing, 39
Rings, flying, 73
Rope climb, 65
Rugby fives goal, 34
Running lanes, 48
Run-up, pole vault, 57

See-saw, 85
Service net, 25
Shot put
    court markings, 26
    men's, 18
    women's, 18
Skittles, 15
Soccer
    ball, 2
    goal, 31
Speedbag, boxing, 38
Speedball goal, 31
Sports wall, 101
Squash, 24, 25
Stakes, horseshoe, 14
Starting blocks, 45
Stopboard, shot put, 18
Swings, 71

Table tennis, 29
Tackling dummy, football, 35
Take-off board, long jump, 53
Tape, finish, 49
Target, archery, 11
Target rings, 7
Target stakes, horsehoe, 14
Teeter-totter, 85·
Tennis
    court dimensions, 8
    rebound net, 12
    rebound wall, 24
    serving distance, 8
    table (Ping-pong), 29
    target ring, 8
Ten-pin bowling, 15
Tetherball, 21
Throwing distance
    baseball, 8
    football, 8
Track and field
    court markings, 26
    discus, 19
    finishing post, 49
    high jump, 54
    hurdles, 51